"K. M. Bascom writes from a heart of passion. As her pastor, I have witnessed her passion for Jesus, her passion for the church, and her passion for the gospel's impact on all nations. So when she asks the question 'Why?', it is more than rhetorical. This work is a heartfelt plea for God's people to understand that the Lord's promise to his chosen people is irrevocable, and that Gentiles will only find God's blessing through the seed of Abraham."

—Dennis Toll
Associate pastor, Grace Baptist Church

"Today Christians are confused by growing polarization, ideological extremism, social divisions, the specter of another world war, and growing antisemitism. Where is history going? Why would God be allowing these rising evils? What does the conflict in Israel have to do with all this? In this day when Christians need a short but informed guide, this little book is a handy introduction. I recommend it to both Christians and Jews."

—Gerald McDermott
Author of *A New History of Redemption: The Work of Jesus the Messiah through the Millennia*

"The history of the relationship between the church and the Jewish people is a huge subject covering nineteen centuries. Over my years of ministry to the Jewish people, I have read many books and articles to learn about this history and still don't know all of it. In her book *Oh, Jew, Oh, Gentile, Why?*, K. M. Bascom has published a concise and accurate summary of this enormous subject from its beginning to the present. I recommend this book to all who want to quickly learn the important points of this subject that has greatly affected world history."

—James Appel
Author of *Appointed Times* series

1

"K. M. Bascom writes with a prophetic voice. She casts the messianic vision in a style few others could. This book gives an insider view of Messianic Judaism. In part, this is because she has read so many other books before writing her own. This enables her to synthesize a wide range of thought. Her informative analysis delves into antisemitism, Jewish history, prophetic Israel, replacement theology, Christian separation from Jewish roots, and many other topics."

—Paul Liberman
President, International Messianic Jewish Alliance

"The latest book by K. M. Bascom could not be more timely or providential. All parties involved in the current crisis in the Middle East are ripe for an insightful assessment of the historical, ethnic, and biblical implications of the millenniums of estrangement among the descendants of Abraham. The author's experience of decades of service in the Middle East, East Africa, and Eastern Europe inculcated with her immersion in Scripture gives us a ray of light into an ever more darkening world."

—Paul E. Barkey
On This Day: A Daily Guide to Spiritual Lessons from American History

Oh Jew,
Oh Gentile,
Why?

Oh Jew,
Oh Gentile,
Why?

Facing Our Estrangement,
Pursuing Biblical Reconciliation

K. M. BASCOM

RESOURCE *Publications* · Eugene, Oregon

OH JEW, OH GENTILE, *WHY?*
Facing Our Estrangement, Pursuing Biblical Reconciliation

Resource Publications
An Imprint of Wipf and Stock Publishers
199 W. 8th Ave., Suite 3
Eugene, OR 97401

www.wipfandstock.com

PAPERBACK ISBN: 979-8-3852-1097-8
HARDCOVER ISBN: 979-8-3852-1098-5
EBOOK ISBN: 979-8-3852-1099-2

VERSION NUMBER 040124

For my Jewish friend,
whose questions have kept me searching
to discover and explain
what has happened to divide
God's Root and Branch people.

Contents

Acknowledgments

Many unmentioned fellow-pilgrims, mentors, authors, and experiences in life have contributed to my burden and equipping for bringing forth this book's concern. For each I am deeply grateful, but I share here only three.

None of my biblical studies would have been written except for the early influence of my first Bible teacher, Bess Combs. She taught us to see the Old and New Testaments (and all history) as one unified story, with the Messiah as its progressive marker and crux. She engendered in me deep respect and appreciation for God's chosen family who gave us God's written Scriptures and Living Word, *Yeshua*/Jesus: incarnated Second Adam, crucified Savior, risen Lord, and eventually returning Bridegroom King.

During the following years, our family was deeply influenced by our repeated times serving in East Africa. Ethiopia is a key Gentile nation brought into God's Jewish family from the time of the Queen of Sheba in the 900s BC, through the Ethiopian official's conversion soon after the Incarnation as told in Acts 8, through King Ezana's conversion in the 300s AD, and to the Solomonic dynasty of the last Emperor of Ethiopia in the 1900s AD. Our faith in the Lord Jesus was immensely deepened by seeing Christ transform the lives of first- and second-generation believers in southern Ethiopia and being challenged by their commitment to speeding the marvelous news of the world's Creator and Savior to other ethnic groups. Witnessing their overcoming faith during Ethiopia's Marxist Revolution further solidified my trust in their Deliverer, and mine.

Most recently, this book could not have emerged without the encouragement and editing assistance of Shelly Potter Larkins, my longtime friend and co-laborer from *The Messiah Mystery* thirty years ago, to this book—undertakings I hadn't enough courage or skill to accomplish without her kindly support and skillful editing.

Ultimately of course, undergirding all the above has been our Creator's revelation of himself to humanity. I so thank him for drawing me to *Yeshua*. I long for God's chosen people and for adopted believers all to choose to love the Savior the Father sent. How blessed we are to enjoy the Spirit's enablement during our earthly pilgrimage, to be brought Home, and then to proceed to adventures in eternity!

Introduction: Dear Reader

Dear Reader, this book is about uncomfortable but crucial questions. Those who are puzzled by shared concerns can be helped by comparing notes. To the sympathetic reader, I am grateful for your understanding. But for those who can sense that the author's assertions are alien or clearly contrary to the reader's viewpoint, why take time to be exposed to this study?

To differing readers, I can only hope that these pages will be informative enough to help clarify the thinking of some with whom you may have disagreed. More importantly, grasping the life-shaping seriousness of the issues could cause us to question our long-held understandings. Only God can judge these things rightly. We who are committed to our Lord need him to bring our thinking and our lives into the unity of the Spirit—not to win arguments, but for our Lord's sake.

This Book's Mode

I am sharing summaries of my research with a broad brush, not as nuanced as a scholarly written treatise. My hope is to bring these concerns to the attention of general readers. The bibliography of studies which have been valuable in my search provides more in-depth sources to those motivated to dig more deeply. While one may not agree with all the listed authors' conclusions, their research and viewpoints can contribute valuable insights.

It would be reasonable for a reader to check out a writer's credentials. Most formative for me has been living daily with the written Word of God for decades. The Old and New Testament tell the unified story of one main character, the Son—the seed of Adam, of Abraham, of David, the divine Word of God, the incarnated Anointed Son. Therefore, the Messiah in both Testaments has been the usual focus of my writings.

An early mentor taught me to approach the Scriptures panoramically, keeping in mind how God's revelation fits together from Genesis to Revelation, from the beginning to the end, from the Alpha to the Omega. That panoramic methodology taught me to patiently look for strands that weave together the perplexities of the Bible, and of life.

Loss of Respectful Listening

Increasingly today, thinking people are sobered by the paralysis of reasonable and respectful consideration of opposite viewpoints. In a typical high school contest, debaters are not told which side of the question they are to defend until they take the stage. They must know the opposing sides of an issue well enough to argue both effectively. But in our post-truth world today, one simple knee-jerk word can bring forth a torrent of judgmental accusation. Those who disagree with one's viewpoint are assumed to be enemies. Evil motivation is quickly ascribed. People are not encouraged to voice a debatable opinion in the public square when alternative viewpoints are called "lies." Being considered a liar does not foster further communication.

The Gift of Written Communication

Writing is one way to communicate without being interrupted or cut short. Of course, written communication means a reader must be willing to participate in this kind of "friendship." Due to my enjoying writer/reader fellowship over the years, biblical writers have become my deeply appreciated friends. Being in Scripture daily teaches us the value of sustained willingness to listen to God.

Who does not ponder the meaning of our own and humanity's pilgrimage? I can only ask readers for charitable willingness to compare my line of thinking to their own. May we take seriously the master key: believing God's awesome disclosures, partial though they be. As 1 Corinthians 13:12 states it: "Now we see but a poor reflection as in a mirror; then we shall see face to face. Now I know in part; then I shall know fully, even as I am fully known." Thanks be to God!

1

Oh Jew, Oh Gentile, *Why?*

Dear Reader, can we agree that our world seems to be floundering in unchartered waters today? Many of us are wondering why. What sort of questions are on the minds of thinking people? Here are a few:

- Why are Jews and the world's Gentile nations perpetually estranged?

- Why haven't education, science, and development brought world peace?

- Why does the world seem to be on the brink of disaster?

- Why is western civilization calling itself "post-Christian"?

- Why is the United States becoming so politically polarized?

- Why are Christians divided over Jewish and Palestinian claims?

- Why is antisemitism rising again in Europe and America?

- Why has the promised return of the Messiah not yet come?

As we ponder such questions, deeper ones arise. Where are we today in humankind's history? What were God's biblical truths and guidelines? What happened to divide us? Where do we see the roots of destructive animosities in history and today?

Who was responsible? How can our ruptures be repaired? Who can reconcile Jews and Gentiles to each other? What deeper understanding of the roots of our estrangements can reduce repercussions within our own faith communities today?

Let's proceed with these questions, as co-searchers, if not allies. We can at least agree that human beings appear to have a thirst for meaning and a yearning for loving relationships. Who has planted these yearnings within us? Since our Creator is infinite and invisible to humans, it seems significant that he used writing as his means to reveal himself and to record humanity's relationship with himself and with each other.

Terminology

To move along our search into his Word, I've provided brief summaries to help unfamiliar readers follow the Bible's unified story. Biblical text locations are given in full, rather than abbreviated.

When we delve into Scripture, we find that God made a noticeable distinction between the family he chose to represent himself, and everyone else in the world. The Hebrews were appointed as the world's "priesthood" (see Exodus 19:6, 40:15). All others in the Bible are either called "the nations" or "the Gentiles." Names are important. Each name represents a whole cluster of personality, life experience, and meanings. Names carry baggage, depending on the name bearer's background. People from various faith communities often use terms that are not well understood by outsiders. Confusion can result as we discuss things of mutual interest. Because we will be considering varying viewpoints, to avoid misunderstanding it would be helpful to clarify how certain words are being used in this book.

Even the terms "Jew" and "Gentile" are sometimes misunderstood. In this study the meaning of "Jewish" indicates descent from the Old Covenant community, the offspring of Abraham, Isaac, and Jacob. "Gentile" is the term for everyone else in the world—i.e., "the nations" ("nation" examples: Isaiah 2:4, 55:5). Note that there can be many columns of biblical references to "nations" in Bible concordances. In the Greek-dominated first century, Paul made the distinction of who he hoped to reach by saying about both groups, "I am obligated both to the Greeks and non-Greeks . . . I am not ashamed of the gospel, because it is the power of God for the salvation of everyone who believes: first for the Jew, then for the Gentile" (Romans 1:14, 16). The two communities are distinguished throughout the Scriptures. Happily, their new union was accomplished by Christ's having made peace between them, as revealed and admonished in Ephesians 2:14–22. And yet, in this union, the distinction between Jew and Gentile remains important, even as the two are made "one new man" (see Ephesians 2:15).

In this study a distinction is made between "Christendom" and Christ. What the Bible says Christ did and said, and what Christendom has done and said, are very different. The repercussions of these aberrations will be explored in what follows.

Among those who identify with Christ, various terms have emerged. For instance, Gentile Christians who do not want to be identified as members of a state-sponsored Orthodox Christian communion, but do follow Jesus, often just call themselves "believers"—meaning believers in Jesus.

Other instances are two terms used for modern Jewish believers in Jesus: "Hebrew Christians" and "Messianic Jews." Before the Holocaust and the rebirth of Israel, Jewish believers in Jesus who became part of churches used to be referred to as "Hebrew Christians." After centuries of persecution and "Christian" Europe's recent genocide of Jews, any of God's chosen people who came to Christ knew that their Jewish community would be totally resistant to anything called "Christian." Some of the hippies in California in the 1970s who became believers during the Jesus Movement were Jewish. When they discovered Jesus to be who he claimed to be, they were puzzled by what to call themselves. Paul Liberman, a lawyer, led a hot debate and finally won. "Messianic Jews" became their designation. Paul recounts the story of that decision in his 2015 book, *Don't Call Me Christian*. However, keep in mind that Messianic Jews *do* believe in *Yeshua*/Christ.

"Church" is another word with multiple meanings. To go back to the Bible, early Christians were called "the saints" (see Ephesians 1:1; Philippians 1:1) or "the church" (see Galatians 1:2; 2 Thessalonians 1:1). Following the Ascension of the Lord, little groups of believers sprang up (as Jesus had predicted) "in Jerusalem, Judea, and in all Samaria, and to the ends of the earth" (Acts 1:8b). These little fellowships were corporately referred to in the New Testament as "the church."

The term "church" did not refer to buildings, denominations, or a hierarchically led organization. "The church" (English) was called the *ekklesia* or *ecclesi*a (Greek and Latin for fellowship), and each smaller group existed as part of the wider *ecclesia*. We need to make a distinction between the church as an invisible living organism, in contrast to visible and countable members of denominations—i.e., organizations such as Catholic, Protestant, or their many derivatives.

In this book, when "church" is capitalized it is meant to refer to the broad, institutionalized Church in the world, in contrast to a simple fellowship or a building.

So, as we proceed in exploring what happened in Christian history, keep in mind the meanings and groupings designated by varying terms: Christendom, Orthodox Jews, Orthodox Christians, Hebrew Christians, Messianic Jews, believers, denominational titles, and more. Terms for Christ will also be expressed by Jesus (English), or *Yeshua* (Hebrew). As printed in Bibles, LORD in capital letters indicates the divine tetragrammaton YHWH (*Yahweh*, the "I Am"), whereas Lord refers to the name *Adonai*.

Our Goal

Why go to all the trouble to examine these confusing facts of history and elements of the faith? The world is wide. Judaism is varied. Christianity is divided. This study's intention is not to champion just one expression of faith. The issues explored are serious. May we all be focusing on our personal response to the actual true living Lord to whom we each must answer.

2

What is the extent of Jew/Gentile alienation?

One way to highlight our world-wide problem is the case of God's chosen people. Contrast Israel's May 14, 2023, celebration of her seventy-five years back in the Jewish homeland (since 1948) with the United Nations General Assembly's resolution to commemorate that day as the seventy-fifth anniversary of the *"Nakba"*—the Arabic word for "catastrophe." The initiative was passed by a vote of ninety in favor, thirty against, and forty-seven abstentions.

Recent Historical Roots

The recent UN vote voicing Israel's nationhood as a catastrophe has an historical/political antecedent that goes back to the European division of Arab areas in 1920. Those losses are still remembered as the Year of Catastrophe in the Arab world, according to James and Marti Hefleys' documentary, *Arabs, Christians, Jews* (118). Researched for many years and published in 1978, their documentary endeavors to give sympathetic and evenhanded reporting of the divergent sociological, historical, and religious strands of all three communities.

For those interested in searching back and exploring our modern problem rooted in the 1800s and 1900s, two valuable books are Larry Collins' and Dominique Laperre's *O, Jerusalem,* published in 1972, and Joan Peters' *From Time Immemorial*, published in 1984.

History of Contempt

While the 2023 UN pronouncement reflects a prevalence of Muslim voters, the influence of wider antisemitism is an historical and present fact. For a scholarly study of Christian culpability, Marvin Wilson's *Our Father Abraham* summarizes Anti-Judaism over the centuries in a chapter titled "A History of Contempt: Anti-Semitism and the Church." After examining its roots and summarizing its terrible repercussions from the first to the twentieth centuries, Wilson calls current Christianity to account:

> We must emphasize in conclusion that the Holocaust did not happen in a vacuum. Though it was devised in a country with an enviable reputation for brilliant culture and intellectual sophistication, the seeds of anti-Semitism had been planted much earlier. The Holocaust represents the tragic culmination of anti-Jewish attitudes and practices which had been allowed to manifest themselves—largely unchecked—in or near the Church for nearly two thousand years. Perhaps the most important reason the Holocaust happened is that the Church had forgotten its Jewish roots. (101)

Blindness to the Jewish People's Anguish

To regard the Holocaust as a latter-day aberration with little roots in the past leaves Christians blind to what a Catholic priest, Edward H. Flannery, calls Christendom to face in his book, *The Anguish of the Jews: Twenty-three Centuries of Antisemitism.* He insists that Christianity's historical ignorance has serious consequences:

> It robs the Christian of grounds for motivation to take hatred of Jews as a serious social and ethical problem

and to discover it in him/herself. It prevents the Christian from understanding Jews, their needs, hurts, and aspirations, many of which were shaped in the crucible of perennial oppression. Further, it blocks the way to Christian self-understanding, for antisemitism has left its mark on the Christian (and his/her church) as much as on the Jew. . . . Of grave consequence, finally, is the fact that this Christian refusal to face the antisemitic past is an important contributor to the extraordinary durability of this longest hatred of human history. (2)

Blind to this historical legacy, today's generation is largely focused on just one inherited issue, the Middle East's impasse, which remains central to the world's present-day instability.

Ancient Resentments and Thereafter

Going back to the struggle's beginning, the book of Genesis reveals the roots of jealousy and resentment that originally arose in the family of Abraham, Isaac, and Jacob. To search back to the ultimate source of rebellion against God's sovereignty, we find Satan's determination to destroy God's fellowship with humans, and they with each other (see Genesis 4:8). Our forefather's second son was killed by the first, a forecast of the future. This deepest history is vital to grasp.

However, this book's study goes only briefly into the deep roots of humanity's tortured scene. Instead, it deals with today's "why" questions related to the divisions which have arisen in the last two thousand years: divisions between Jews and Jews, Jews and Gentiles, Gentiles and Gentiles, and especially Christians versus Christians today.

Although most Gentiles today are unaware of this reality, Jews have been persecuted, defrauded, exiled, and executed over and over in the last two thousand years. Christian rulers gave Jews just three options: conversion, exile, or death. Those who refused to convert faced repeated mass expulsions. In his 2020 book, *The Eternal People,* the Dutch theologian and philosopher Willem J. Ouweneel documents how widely expulsion from Christian nations occurred:

> In 1290, the Jews were expelled from England. In 1306, they were expelled from France, and in 1492 the massive expulsion of the Jews from Spain occurred. There were many expulsions, throughout the centuries, from German-speaking and Eastern European countries. (143)

The counterpart to driving them out was the refusal to let them in. Ouweneel reports what people today may not realize, that between 1920 and 1939, the Americans had a policy in which the flight of the European Jews to the United States was actively impeded. He theorizes:

> If the Nazis killed almost six million Jews, this high number could have been reached because countries like the United States, Great Britain, Switzerland, and others refused to admit Jews who wished to flee from rising and threatening Nazism. In this way, such countries unconsciously cooperated in the Holocaust. (144)

European "Christian" Gentiles in various countries repeatedly ghettoed or exiled this unique people, declaring "You have no right to live among us." Hitler pushed it further, devising his final solution: "You have no right to live." To grasp the vast organization of the Nazi means of destruction, see Raul Hilberg's 778-page documentation, *The Destruction of the European Jews*.

After the Nazi's systematic genocide, the long-time advocacy of a minority of concerned Christians on the one hand, and European guilt on the other, led to the Jewish people being allowed in 1948 to escape to a tiny area that had originally been their God-ordained homeland (see Genesis 15:18–20; Nehemiah 9:8, 15, 23). Strangely, one wonders whether their return to statehood could have happened without the impetus of the despicable Holocaust.

Israel's Challenging Internal Divides

Those who escaped to Israel came from various countries and with differing motivations, some to develop the new nation as secular kibbutzniks and others afire as religious Zionists. Yossi Klein Halevi helps readers realize this deep problem in his book initiated by the 1967 Six-Day War: *Like Dreamers: The Story of the Israeli Paratroopers Who Reunited Jerusalem and Divided a Nation.* The heart-rending conceptual divides between secular and religious Israelites that the book so skillfully portrays are at the boiling point within Israeli society today.

The Israeli and Palestinian Enigma

Facing our contemporary situation, after years of suffering and negotiations, no solution has emerged. For those on the outside, windows into Arab and Israeli lives are poignantly revealed in heart-rending testimonies, one from Muslim background, the other Jewish. *Son of Hamas* by Mosab Hassan Yousef reveals the toll of Arab hatred as viewed through the angst-ridden pilgrimage of a ten-year Palestinian double agent, the son of a top leader of Hamas. *Letters to my Palestinian Neighbor* by Yossi Klein Halevi is a Jewish citizen's poignant plea for human understanding across Israel's tragic political divide. Halevi writes:

> Instead, we're trapped in what may be called a "cycle of denial." Your side denies my people's legitimacy, my right to self-determination, and my side prevents your people from achieving national sovereignty. The cycle of denial defines our shared existence, an impossible intimacy of violence, suppression, rage, despair. That is the cycle we can only break together. (115–116)

These insider descriptions help outsiders understand and empathize with the suffering of both communities.

For a Gentile trying to understand the complicated West Bank situation, see *The Mountains of Israel: The Bible and the West Bank* by Norma Parrish Archbold. (The mountains of

Israel are Judea and Samaria.) This small book is a helpful primer with simplified maps, facts, and illustrations. It has been repeatedly translated and is available in seven languages. For another viewpoint, Adi Schwarts in *The War of Return* blames the UNRWA's perpetuation of refugee status as a major contributor to the ongoing entanglement. (When the United Nations Relief and Works Agency began in 1950, there were 750,000 Palestinian refugees. Today, there are 5.9 million eligible for UNRWA services in multiple countries.)

Betrayals and attacks have continually dogged this Jewish "nation born in a day" (Isaiah 66:8a)—a day just seventy-five years ago. On that historic day, President Harry Truman dared to affirm Jewish nationhood by the United States. God's chosen people continue to find themselves surrounded by Middle Eastern enemies who openly vow to destroy her, and even deny Israel's right to exist. Those who have not inherited centuries of the Middle East's exchange of offenses and retaliations can hardly fathom such a united dismissal of a whole nation's existence.

Sudden Horrific Attack

During this book's writing, on October 7, 2023, exactly fifty years after being attacked on Yom Kipper of 1973, Israel was viciously attacked yet again, this time on the Feast of Sukkot's holiest day. The perpetrators used suffering Palestinians as their pawns as they set off a whole conflagration now diabolically unraveling in the Middle East, and beyond.

Why, World, Why?

How can it be that the existence of one nation in the world, one special people's small historic homeland, should be considered the world's major problem? When we delve into the history of all this animosity, we are puzzled at its genocidal repetitions over the ages: Egypt, Persia, Rome, Middle Ages, Christendom,

Hitler, and today's repeatedly avowed completion of "the final solution." Has the majority of the world so summarily rejected their Creator, the God of Abraham, Isaac, and Jacob, that they also reject his chosen people? Are those who were destined to bring forth his Messiah's redemption for the world allowed no place on earth? If so, why?

Outsiders' Implication

Lest outsiders stand aloof in cultural smugness, in reality all of us are participating in the repercussions of this conflict, however well or how little we understand the roots of Israel's suffering. Eric Metaxas wrote his earlier book, *Bonhoeffer,* in 2010 about Dietrich Bonhoeffer's leadership of the Confessing Church's resistance in Germany. Metaxas documents the German state Church's complicity with the Nazis' "final solution." In his 2022 book, *Letter to the American Church,* Metaxas sees most American churches' acquiescence to today's cultural trends as resembling the compliant German church in the 1930s (17). This parallel is a dead serious warning.

Within Christendom there are stark divisions today over Israel's right to her homeland. Israel's mysterious survival comes as a supernaturally delivered amazement to some, and as a theological embarrassment to others. How can those with opposing viewpoints understand each other?

In his comprehensive documentary, *"The Anguish of the Jews,"* Edward H. Flannery exclaims, "The very magnitude of the record, seen as a whole, cries out for explanation. How did this amalgam of undying hatred and oppression come to be? What is it essentially? Who or what was responsible?" (284). In over eleven pages he analyzes a host of possible and nuanced answers to these questions—historical, psychological, theological, subliminal, and more. Although he hopes to confront Christian antisemitism with an urgent call for repentance, this is his diagnosis:

> The indifference affecting the subject is attributable in the first place to the all but total ignorance of Christians as to what happened to Jews in Christian history and the extent of the involvement of the Church and the Church's teachings. The tale told in this book is still a missing page in our Christian histories and texts. Until it is reinserted, the apathy and general lack of motivation will continue, as will by consequence the longest hatred in history. (295)

While Flannery does reference the Apostle Paul's teachings in the New Testament about Jewish and Gentile relationships, he does not seem to go back to the Old Testament reference that would be the actual "longest hatred in history." Documented in Genesis, the hatred resident in God's enemy, Satan, incited hatred of God in humankind at the Fall. If we take Scripture seriously, we realize that hatred of God became an underlying sin in the human heart. It surfaces in many forms, both secular and religious. Our Creator God's chosen representatives—his prophets and even his Son—were resisted, hated, and killed throughout history. Consider *Yeshua's* pronouncement, "He who hates me hates my Father as well" (John 15:23). We would all do well to check our own hearts.

3

How have Jews and Gentiles diverted from God's ordained patterns?

Our world's escalating catastrophes cause us to wonder what our independent man-made decisions, traditions, and actions have reaped. How have we diverted from our Creator's guidelines for the well-being of humanity? The burden of this book calls Jews and Gentiles to look at our shared history from God's perspective. The only authoritative revelation of his perspective is the Word of God: history's baseline and plumb line.

Recalling the Old Testament's Saga

For the sake of readers with less biblical background, it seems helpful to provide a brief review of early Jewish and Christian history. Apologetically, this is a broad-brush overview. Scriptural references are provided so that the summaries may be investigated.

The Torah records God's sovereign choice of Israel, and the history of their relationship with Him. Moses reminds the chosen people:

> For you are a people holy to the LORD your God. The LORD your God has chosen you out of all the peoples on the face of the earth to be his people, his treasured

possession. The LORD did not set his affection on you and choose you because you were more numerous than other peoples, for you were the fewest of all peoples. But it was because the LORD loved you and kept the oath he swore to your forefathers that he brought you out with a mighty hand and redeemed you from the land of slavery, from the power of Pharoah king of Egypt. Know therefore that the LORD your God is God: he is the faithful God, keeping his covenant of love to a thousand generations of those who love him and keep his commands. (Deuteronomy 7:6–9)

If we search back to Israel's forefather, we come to Abraham. God's plan was to call Abraham's family to bless the world, promising him that "all the peoples on earth will be blessed through you" (Genesis 12:3b). If we follow the Messianic line through Isaac, Jacob, and Joseph, we come eventually to Moses and Israel's Egyptian bondage for four hundred years. Finally, God delivered them miraculously across the Red Sea and into the Sinai desert. The LORD began forming this multitude who had been living as slaves into his own plan for their destiny. He revealed to Moses his overall patterns for their living: their sustenance, their worship, their moral guidelines, and their calendar. Then he sent them to settle in a small area where they were to replace tribes whom God had waited those four hundred years to judge for their lustful idol worship of Baal and Ashtoreth, and child sacrifice to Molech (see Genesis 15:13–16; Leviticus 18:24–28).

The LORD called the descendants of Abraham, Isaac, and Jacob to be his kingdom of priests and a holy nation among all the nations, the Gentiles (see Exodus 19:6). The Old Testament's historical books record the successes and failures of Israel to be faithful to their God. Biblical heroes' flaws are not hidden. God's Word speaks truth honestly.

The LORD eventually revealed Jerusalem to be their center, the long promised "place the Lord thy God shall choose"

(Deuteronomy 12:5, 11, 14, 18, etc.). Soon after the height of their kingdom's glory at the time of King David's and Solomon's United Kingdom, ten tribes split off from Judah, and only Judah and Benjamin remained centered in Jerusalem. With more evil kings than faithful, both kingdoms' practice of obedience was rare. The ten northern tribes became increasingly idolatrous, so God allowed Assyrians to attack and scatter them abroad. Judah and Benjamin in the south remained, but also fell into idolatry, bringing judgment that destroyed their Temple and sent them to a seventy-year exile called "the Babylonian captivity." Eventually, as prophesied, Cyrus allowed the captive Jews to return to Jerusalem, build a second temple and recalibrate. Growing insincerity of worship brought reproof through God's prophets. After little repentance, no more prophets arose in Israel. Following four hundred years of prophetic silence, God spoke again through the Incarnation.

Summarizing the New Testament Saga

The Incarnation takes us to the record of the Messiah, who for three years preached, healed, and raised the dead. He was crucified on a Roman cross, physically rose from the grave, and poured out the Spirit of God in such power that *Yeshua's* fearful disciples were transformed into ambassadors of the Jewish Messianic hope's fulfillment. In the first few decades of the first century AD, nearly all members of the believing community were Jewish. Their only Bible was the Hebrew Bible, and when the New Covenant was put in writing, the Spirit of God inspired only apostolic Jews to be its authors, except perhaps one Gentile, Luke. The New Testament's first four books chronicle the Messiah's life, death, and resurrection. Then the Book of Acts records how the Gospel spread to Gentiles. The Letters explain God's grace and ways to new believers. Finally, the future is predicted in Revelation. The whole Bible was written by Jews and to Jews. From the book of Acts on, Gentile believers who were grafted into Israel were also addressed.

The Role of Prophecy

As we consider divergence from God's truth, false prophets were an early form of that blight. One of the key factors built into the scriptures was the function of prophecy. God had ordained that his priests would represent man to God, and his prophets would represent God to man. God's prophets were both *forth* tellers (messengers) and *fore*tellers (predicters). However, false prophets were always a problem. God's standard to prove his own true prophets' authenticity was simply whether their predicted "Thus saith the Lord" proved true. Throughout the Old Testament, God revealed future happenings through his prophets, and then their fulfillments were recorded. However, when God sent his Son to earth, *Yeshua* never prefaced his words with: "Thus saith the Lord," but always spoke with divine authority: "I say . . ." The biblical test for authenticity was clearly demonstrated by *Yeshua's* repeated predictions that he would be crucified but would rise from the grave. His Resurrection overwhelmingly proved *Yeshua's* authenticity and his identity. It became the core of witness to the amazing "Good News" offered to humanity, "the Gospel" (see Romans 1:15–16).

Fulfillment: The Key to Authenticity

Foretelling-type prophecy (prediction and fulfillment) is one of the bridges between the two covenants. *Yeshua* made his purpose clear, saying, "Do not think that I have come to abolish the Law or the Prophets: I have not come to abolish them but to fulfill them" (Matthew 5:17). In the New Testament, in all four Gospels, dozens of references point out aspects of *Yeshua's* life and sacrificial death as fulfillments of Old Testament prophecies, explaining, "This was to fulfill . . . " (quoting Isaiah, Jeremiah, David, Zechariah, Malachi, and others). Peter quotes

Joel at Pentecost. Paul's letters repeatedly appeal to the writings of Moses, David, Hosea, and Isaiah.

The Old and New Testaments are inseparably integrated. Notice the continuity of the community of faith from Abraham forward, and even beyond the Incarnation. All were Jewish. Not understanding the relationship between the two covenants has caused huge relational problems over the centuries! The biblical attitude toward both the Old and New Testaments is deeply respectful, intertwined, and successive. The two could be pictured as the first and second floor of the same home. The lower story is the foundation from which the upper story rises. Either one is incomplete without the other. If the foundation is missing, the upper structure has no firm base. If the upper structure is absent, the crowning fulfillment is lacking. Either one alone stands exposed "without a roof." The roof is God's eternal purpose displayed in its full glory.

God's Actual Words

We should not take for granted Scriptures' rare accounts of the miracle of *hearing* God's voice, or centuries later, our gift of *reading* his messages. God's own words—the Scriptures—are his peoples' foundation for living. The Father's words guided Israel. The Son's agreeing words and redeeming work fulfilled the Scriptures. Then the Spirit continued God's presence on earth. The Holy Spirit's inspiration brought forth the New Testament's four testimonies to the Lord's life, teachings, healings, miracles, warnings, and commands in the Gospels. Acts tells us how the gospel spread; the Letters deal with basic foundations for the early church; and Revelation predicts what will happen at the end of the age.

Yeshua's Uncomplicated Mode

In contrast to the religious practices of the day, Jesus set up no new hierarchical leadership, no status differentiation. He came in humility to serve, and his followers were also to simply serve. Theirs would be a different kind of priesthood. In Moses' time, God had told Israel, "Although the whole earth is mine, you will be for me a kingdom of priests and a holy nation" (Exodus 19:6). Now God and his incarnated Son were widening their invitation of salvation to the whole world. All those who trusted in Jesus would become a full "priesthood of believers" (see 1 Peter 2:5, 9; Revelation 1:6). *Yeshua* knew that the Temple worship would be over soon. He, Isaiah 53's Lamb of God, would actually be the final sacrifice.

Amazingly, Jesus summarized the Law in just two commandments (see Matthew 22:37–39). He spoke of only two ordinances—baptism (see Matthew 28:19) and the Lord's Supper (see Luke 22:19, 20; 1 Corinthians 11:23–26). He gave just one new commandment—"love one another" (see John 15:12), and only one commission—to offer the gift of salvation to the whole world (see Matthew 28:18–20). He left the rest up to his replacement, the Spirit's leading!

Most crucial to Jesus was people's realizing the fundamental fact that his authority came from his identity—from who he was. Near to his impending sacrifice, *Yeshua* questioned his men about who people thought he was. "'But what about you?' he asked. 'Who do you say I am?' Simon Peter answered, 'You are the Christ, the Son of the living God'" (Matthew 16:15–16). "Christ" means Messiah. *Yeshua* affirmed that this would be the rock on which he would build his church. He himself knew that his church—his body of believers—would not all be Jewish, but would so spread out into the world that finally there would be representatives from every tribe and nation at his throne (see Revelation 5:9, 7:9).

The Savior's Successor?

Jesus admonished Peter to shepherd the flock, but it is significant that the Lord of the church did not appoint a human successor. Instead, he promised the arrival of a divine replacement. The Holy Spirit would not be limited to one time or place but would bring Jesus' very presence into the life of any true believer.

As Scripture affirms, "For the law was given through Moses; grace and truth came through Jesus Christ" (John 1:17). Moses had been God's deliverer of Israel from physical bondage. *Yeshua* is God's deliverer of the world from spiritual bondage. Israel's Messianic hope was high in Jewish thought near the time of the Incarnation, although the main expectation was for a military deliverer who would free them from Rome. The true Messiah came to free all mankind from the universal sin problem that separates us from God.

Man-Made Traditions

Israel's teachers of the law and Pharisees had added a host of rules to God's original commandments for right living. *Yeshua* called them to account, saying, "You nullify the word of God for the sake of your traditions" (Matthew 15:6).

Similarly, throughout the centuries, man-made additions and substitutions have done great damage to both Jews and Gentiles trying to live out their faith. Christian clerics since the Messiah's Incarnation also have nullified the word of God for the sake of man-made traditions, traditions sometimes created to promote their own power. (Chapter 8 focuses on these deviations.) The Reformation in the 1500s stood against many of these abuses, but some remain. To summarize, although there have been godly exceptions, many things have not gone well for Israel in her two-thousand-year history before the Incarnation, nor for the Church in these two thousand years afterward. The following material will try to especially recognize Christendom's failures, because they impinge upon our present situation.

When we look at our predicament today, reviewing our ancestors' history can be revealing. We are cut from the same

Adamic nature as theirs, with the same rebellious attitudes, and the same proclivities to sin. In the material that follows we will look at how Christendom also faltered, partially missed its calling, and how some of its leadership also fell into hypocrisy. There is plenty of criticism to go around whenever we look at the history of humanity, Jewish or Gentile though we may be.

We all seem to have diverted from God's ordained patterns for harmonious and blessed living. It would be wise to go back to the foundations laid by the One who created us, loves us dearly, offers us forgiveness, and redeems anyone who responds to his love.

4

What were God's guidelines for transformed Jew/Gentile relationships?

One of the problems in the current debate over the Holy Land is the lack of biblical and historical perspective on the part of both Muslims and Christians. The world resents God's choice of a single nation through which to begin to work, not knowing or appreciating God's goal at the call of Abraham, that "all peoples on earth will be blessed through you" (Genesis 12:3b). Humanity continues to echo Satan's rebellion-designed question, "Did God really say . . . ?" (see Genesis 3:1).

"Chosenness"

Rather than beginning with how we see our situation today, we could orient our exploration by asking questions such as, "What does all this 'chosenness' mean to God? How does it fit into his sovereign plan for the world's redemption?"

A "chosen son" has always been resented—whether Abel, Abraham, Isaac, Jacob, Joseph, David, or the ultimate Son, Jesus. "Israel" stands for them all. The Creator's "chosen" are hated by God's enemy, Satan. Only the demonic could be behind the genocidal atrocities to which they have been subjected—in Pharoah's Egypt, Haman's Persia, Herod's Rome, Rome's legions, in "Christian" Europe, in the Holocaust, and in the Middle East's and Christendom's partial animosity today. Furthermore, not only the Creator's chosen people but his chosen *land* ups the increment of resentment.

One People's Separation in the Torah

The Old Testament records how God established the foundation for his chosen people's relationships with himself and with each other. Genesis gives us the priceless history of humanity's beginning. Exodus gives us God's Ten Commandments, laying out principles for harmonious living: worship the Creator, rest every seventh day, honor family, live in marital fidelity, do not murder, lie, steal, or covet—a blessed culture! Leviticus, Numbers, and Deuteronomy go on to record the establishment and history of the community from which the Messiah would eventually come.

Hebrew History

The opening chapters of Chronicles record the family lines of the twelve tribes of Israel. The historical books take us to Israel's priesthood, early prophets, and the kingship. God promised King David an ongoing kingship, the reason the Messiah would later be called "the Son of David," "the greater David," the "Lion of Judah." The monarchy split in two. Successive kings largely did evil. A few, especially Josiah and Hezekiah, brought in reforms. Due to their idol worship, God allowed Israel in the north to be decimated by the Assyrians. Soon Judah's idol worship in the south also brought God's judgement, causing them to go into captivity. Seventy years later, delegations of Jews returned from Babylon and rebuilt Jerusalem's altar, Temple, and wall. Devotion to the LORD rose, then waned, although empty rituals remained.

The Incarnation

After four hundred years with no prophetic voice, a prophet named John called Israel to repentance and was baptizing crowds at the Jordan River. John was the forerunner, the "Elijah," who introduced *Yeshua*, proclaiming, "Behold the Lamb of God who takes away the sin of the world" (John 1:29). God's process for offering redemption to all humanity had come to its fulfillment in the approaching sacrifice of the Lamb of God for the entire world.

Jews and the nations (Gentiles) had been kept separate during the time that the ancestry of the Messiah had to remain intact. But once he came, he opened the grace of God to the whole world. That actuality was demonstrated by the thick curtain in the Temple splitting open from top to bottom at the moment when the Messiah cried out from the cross, "It is finished!" (John 19:30a). Thereafter, all humanity has been invited to come boldly to the throne of Grace (see Hebrew 4:16).

Yeshua's ancestry authenticated God's promises to Abraham, Isaac, Jacob, and David. His identity was vindicated by the Resurrection. Yet, as predicted in Isaiah 53, Israel's Messiah was despised and rejected. As the Apostle John reported it:

> He came to that which was his own, but his own did not receive him. Yet to all who received him, he gave the right to become children of God—children born not of natural descent, not of human decision or a husband's will, but born of God. The Word became flesh and made his dwelling among us. We have seen his glory, the glory of the One and Only, who came from the Father, full of grace and truth. (John 1:11–14)

Repeatedly, Jesus told his disciples that he would soon be crucified but that he would be resurrected on the third day (see Matthew 16:21; Mark 8:31; Luke 9:22). They did not understand this strange prediction. But three days after his crucifixion,

Yeshua's promise of his defeat over death actually came true (see Matthew 28; Mark 16; Luke 24; John 20–21).

The Revelation at Pentecost

Recorded in the fourteenth chapter of the Gospel of John, Jesus had explained that his bodily presence on earth, limited in time and place, would be replaced by the provision of the Holy Spirit to indwell all who received him. The Spirit would be unhindered by physical limitations. He would point them to the Savior and empower believers to be his ambassadors to the world. Before his ascension, the risen Christ told his people to wait in Jerusalem, for the Spirit would soon be poured out on believers.

Acts 2 records what happened when Christ's prophecy came true fifty days after the Resurrection at the Feast of Weeks, now called Pentecost. The Spirit revealed a mystery—something previously unknown: "This mystery is that through the gospel the Gentiles are heirs together with Israel, members together of one body, and sharers together in the promise in Christ Jesus" (Ephesians 3:6). Thereafter, a band of Jews began spreading a whole new dynamic of joy out over the world.

The Jerusalem Council (Acts 15)

Soon Gentiles too were believing and worshiping God through *Yeshua*. That phenomenon proved to be a whole new problem for the Jewish believers to face. Acts 15 gives us an account of their Jerusalem Council, when a decision was made that changed the world. What was to be done about all these believing Gentiles, ungodly people whom Jews had always avoided? The Jewish believers' leaders called a council and heard accounts from Peter, Paul, and Barnabas about the Spirit of God falling on Gentiles just as on Jews on the day of Pentecost. In the New Testament book of Acts, the Holy Spirit records the process by which God convinced the Jewish leaders to accept the Savior's gift of salvation not only for themselves, but potentially for the rest of the world. "Old and new wineskins, both to be preserved," is what Jesus had called these two groups (see Matthew 9:17). Paul explained that Gentiles were "foreigners and aliens to be accepted into the household of God" (see Ephesians 2:19–22). Letting the rule of circumcision be omitted for Gentile followers of *Yeshua,* the Jewish leadership decided on just three principles to protect Gentile converts and to anticipate Jewish dietary rules related to eating together. They were directed to stay sexually pure, reject idol worship, and respect guidelines related to meat and blood (see Acts 15:28–29). Eating with a Gentile had formerly been forbidden to a Jew.

Dissentions and Reversal

For the first Jewish *Yeshua* followers, living in fellowship with Gentiles was extremely difficult to accept. A whole group called the Circumcision opposed this openness vehemently. They insisted that Gentiles had to be circumcised and keep the law (i.e., become Jews) before they could be accepted as Christians. The Jerusalem Council reluctantly, but obediently to the Spirit, had decided the case by accepting God's indication that Gentiles did not need to become Jews to be accepted into the household of faith.

Regrettably, a couple centuries later, the opposite decision was made. Jews were required to become Gentiles (relinquish Sabbath keeping and all things Jewish) to be considered Christians. That misguided and violently enforced decision was not in tune with the Spirit, and proved disastrous for Jews, for the Gospel, and for the authenticity of God-ordained fellowship. We reap its consequences today.

The Risen Christ's Deployment of Paul

Soon after the Lord's earthly sojourn, a Pharisee named Saul had been decimating the Church. When traveling to Damascus, Saul was suddenly confronted by *Yeshua,* who commissioned him with the task of taking the Gospel to the Gentiles, an incomprehensible assignment for an Orthodox Jew (see Acts 9:1–18). By the Spirit's enabling, Saul (later known by his Greek name Paul) did obey Jesus by pouring out his life for the Gentiles. But he testified in Romans 9:1 that he continually had "great sorrow and anguish of heart" over the unbelief of "my brothers, those of my own race."

> Theirs is the adoption as sons; theirs is the divine glory, the covenants, the receiving of the law, the temple worship, and the promises. Theirs are the patriarchs, and from them is traced the human ancestry of Christ, who is God over all, forever praised! Amen. (Romans 9:4b–5)

Root and Branch Relationships

When Paul wrote the letter to Roman Christians, he was addressing a believing community that was a mixture of Jews scattered to Rome and first-generation believing Gentiles. In chapters 9–11 of Paul's letter to Rome, he wisely advised this mixed community to be careful how they understood and treated each other. He addressed Gentile believers with a basic truth and a stern warning:

> If some of the branches have been broken off, and you, though a wild olive shoot, have been grafted in among the others and now share in the nourishing sap from the olive root, do not boast over those branches. If you do, consider this: You do not support the root, but the root supports you. (Romans 11:17–18)

Paul's letter to the largely Gentile Ephesian believers gives us God's marvelous provision for Jew/Gentile relationships:

> Therefore, remember that formerly you who are Gentiles by birth and called "uncircumcised" by those who call themselves "the circumcision" (that done in the body by the hands of men)—remember that at that

time you were separate from Christ, excluded from
citizenship in Israel and foreign to the covenants of the
promise, without hope and without God in the world.
But now in Christ Jesus you who were once far away
have been brought near through the blood of Christ
. . . His purpose was to create in himself one new man
out of the two, thus making peace, and in this one body
to reconcile both of them through the cross, by which
he put to death their hostility. (Ephesians 2:11–13, 15b,
16)

Sadly, however, for nearly two thousand years, Gentiles have
not treated Jews as biblically directed, right down to our own
century. In light of Scripture, how could this have happened?
Recognizing the dreadful persecution of Jewish communities
and trying to trace its causes is urgent for today's generation of
Gentiles to humbly and responsibly pursue.

5

What happened with Jews and Gentiles in the first century after the Incarnation?

After Pentecost, when the Spirit began to indwell believers (see Acts 2:33), Jesus' eleven disciples who had been in hiding were suddenly transformed into bold witnesses. Filled with the Spirit, Peter was given the explanation of the tongues of fire from the prophecy of Joel. After he spoke, three thousand people believed (see Acts 2:41). Day by day more Jews in Jerusalem believed. Their number grew to five thousand (see Acts 4:4). The Pharisees were livid. When Stephen spoke so bluntly to them, they stoned him to death (see Acts 7).

Scattering Persecution

Thereafter, great persecution broke out against *Yeshua* believers, and they were scattered throughout Judea and Samaria. Wherever they went, new people believed. Jesus had told them they would be his witnesses "in Jerusalem, Judea, Samaria, and to the ends of the earth." (Acts 1:8b) The Ethiopian official to whom Philip was sent on the Gaza Road became the first representative of those being reached "to the ends of the earth" (see Acts 8:26–40). Originally thought of as a Jewish sect in

Jerusalem, believers in *Yeshua* began to be called "Christ-ones/ Christians" in the Gentile city of Antioch (see Acts 11:26).

The Exactitude of the Apostolic Letters

This openness to the whole world was a huge shock to the Jewish people and was not easily accepted. The Spirit of God had to establish the reality of salvation's widened scope through letters sent to various congregations. The New Testament records twenty-one of these letters from the Apostles Paul, Peter, and John, plus James and Jude, Jesus' half-brothers who believed only after the Resurrection of *Yeshua*. Repeatedly these apostolic communications warned against false teachers, especially the Judaizers who demanded circumcision, and the Gnostics who separated body and spirit and propagated false interpretations.

These early apostolic letters kept explaining, teaching, clarifying, and correcting first generation churches. The Spirit used these careful guidelines to establish the basics of biblical faith that we also need. Their exactitude in the New Testament reminds us of God's command to Moses to build the Tabernacle "exactly according to the pattern" (see Exodus 25:9, 40). Why so exactly? Because that pattern would be repeated in the Temple and would be used to communicate the basic tenants of Judaism throughout the Old Testament. Its elements: The Bronze Altar for substitutional sacrifice, the Laver for cleansing, the Menorah for light, the Showbread for fellowship, the Altar of Incense for prayer, the Ark containing the broken law, God's Throne of Grace above the Ark, where the atoning blood would "cover" the broken law below. Each element's meanings would eventually emerge in the coming Messiah's life and teachings, and they would provide platforms for his proclamations at the Feasts. Those "exact" and all-revealing elements would demonstrate his fulfillment of *being* all that the patterns had represented. The Savior's use of the divine "I AMs" revealed his biblically exact fulfillments of God's patterns. The Lamb of God claimed, "I AM the way, I am the light of the world; I AM the Bread from heaven; Mine is the blood of atonement."

Both Together Created to be "One New Man" in Christ

New Gentile believers needed to be taught the Old Testament Scriptures, the foundation of Christian faith. In addition, these "aliens" especially had to be taught how precious and accepted they were to God. Paul's letter to the Ephesians in Asia Minor speaks authoritatively about this newly provided acceptance.

> Consequently, you are no longer foreigners and aliens, but fellow citizens with God's people and members of God's household, built on the foundation of the apostles and prophets, with Christ Jesus himself as the chief cornerstone. (Ephesians 2:19–20)

Making it clear in Scripture, the Spirit of God enabled Jews and Gentiles to accept each other in the early days of what came to be called "the church"—not a building, but scattered home-hosted fellowships.

The First Century Situation

Trying to comprehend this situation in its historical context, we can attempt to put ourselves in the shoes of "the church" fellowship in Rome in the sixties AD. A number of Jewish people had gone to Rome for business, and others due to persecution that had scattered them. Rome ruled much of the world. The Temple was still standing in Jerusalem, and the Sanhedrin was still in charge. The resurrection of the Savior was at the heart of the good news that Christians were spreading. The Jewish leadership tried to negate this astounding miracle. They had bribed the regiment they had sent to watch the tomb to say that the Disciples stole the body of Jesus while the whole regiment was asleep (see Matthew 28:11–15). Remember that no one ever found the supposed body, and ten of *Yeshua's* disciples eventually died martyrs' deaths for testifying absolutely that they and others had repeatedly met and even eaten with the Savior during the forty days after his Resurrection, before his Ascension.

More Martyrs

In Rome there would have been both unbelieving Orthodox Jews and *Yeshua*-believing Jews, and there would have been enmity between them. The believing Jewish remnant was resisted by both unbelieving Jews and the ruling Roman Gentiles. *Foxe's Book of Martyrs* records Nero's demented torching of Christians and round after round of persecution that followed. How beleaguered but united this little band of Jewish and Gentile Christians must have been in that era when the Apostle Paul and possibly Peter were executed in Rome!

In AD 70 the Romans destroyed the Temple and left Jerusalem in ruins. That ended all atoning sacrifices and dispersed the priesthood. To completely crush the Jews, another Roman invasion in AD 72–73 assaulted a high mesa fortress built by Herod, where nearly one thousand Jews, rather than being taken captive, all committed suicide. "Masada never again!" is a Jewish vow.

Then Came Constantine

The Roman Empire's persecution of Christians continued up to the 300s AD. Then with Constantine, everything changed. Although touted as a first Christian emperor, Constantine launched a bowling ball down history that did severe damage to both Jews and Gentiles. It will be revealing next to examine this emperor's influence and trace the weighty repercussions that affect us deeply even today.

6

Who "Gentile-ized" the church and set up contradictions that still divide Christians?

We look at the fractured nature of Judeo/Christian relationships today and wonder how all the splintering started. The Jew and Gentile "one new man" relationship (see Ephesians 2:15) revealed by the Holy Spirit began to be either forgotten or ignored. By the 300s AD, the early relationship between Jewish and Gentile believers was being turned on its head.

The Jerusalem Council's Principles Inverted

To review: In compliance with the Jerusalem Council that had been held in the fifties AD, early Jewish Christians had graciously decided not to require Gentile believers to convert to Judaism to be accepted as Christians (see Acts 15). But a couple centuries later when Gentiles outnumbered Jewish believers in Jesus, Gentile churchmen began requiring Jews to conform to Gentile-ized society. In Rome, Jews were forbidden to keep the Sabbath or to celebrate their God-ordained feasts, covenantal practices that God had commanded his people to pass on to every generation. A diabolical reversal was taking place. Jews were essentially being told they had to become Gentiles to be accepted as Christians. After all, it was reasoned, the Temple was gone, Jerusalem was destroyed, and Jews were scattered out of the Holy Land. Their season seemed to be over. The Church assumed it had replaced and superseded Israel. Taking this crucial reversal into account, we begin to grasp why Christendom became so blighted. Child was renouncing and separating from parent.

Roadblocks to Redemption

This rejection led to an alienation that has perpetually injured the Jewish people, pushing them out of the means of grace. Jonathan Bernis, a Messianic Jew in our generation, termed these erroneous viewpoints "Roadblocks to Redemption," the title of his article in the Sept./Oct. 2008 *Jewish Voice* magazine. He appealed to Romans 1:16's mandate to proclaim the gospel "to the Jew first." On the article's first page, the carved stone face of the Roman emperor Constantine stares at the reader.

Why Constantine? This emperor brought forth the birth of what we call "Christendom." He changed the face of Christianity. The story of this man's influence is intricately documented in a repeatedly published book by A. H. M. Jones, *Constantine and the Conversion of Europe.* The author gives a detailed account, but to summarize, when Constantine and a rival were vying for the leadership of Rome in AD 312, Constantine had a vision of a cross in the sky with the words "in this sign conquer." He won the battle. Thereafter, the cross became his insignia in battle, as well as in battles of later generations. Using a cross in war was completely incongruent to the meaning of *Yeshua's* peace-making blood shed on the cross. Constantine's victory led him to legalize Christianity. This may have led to the mistaken assumption that his newly Christianized empire was the kingdom of God on earth, fulfilling the prophecy of an eternal kingdom in Daniel 2:44–45.

Constantine's powerfully significant influence changed the face of Christianity in three main ways: it opened the door to the union of church and state; it re-defined the nature of the Church; and it initiated the Church's use of the sword.

To recognize this church/state theocratic aberration, we need to compare it with the biblical pattern. Jesus had activated no union with ruling authorities, neither sacred nor political. When the Gospel was spreading, those individuals who believed in the Lord Jesus and made their decision public by baptism were eventually called "Christians." We take this pattern for granted, but at that time personal choice was actually a revolutionary way to think of how a believing community could be constituted. The biblical *ecclesia* known as "the church" is an invisible living organ*ism*, not a visible, countable, controllable organi*zation*. Scripturally speaking, no one can be *born* a Christian, as in other religions. Jesus invited people to be *reborn* by personal choice and the work of the Holy Spirit (see John 3:1–16).

"Sacralism" Altered the Church

Constantine's expectation that all of his realm follow the emperor's religion was a generally accepted concept. Unified government and religion remain the expectation in much of our world today. Whether we think of "Dianna of the Ephesians," or "Baal of the Amorites," or "Allah of the Muslims," most countries think even today that "to be a ____ is to be ____." Sacr*al* (i.e., not sacr*ed*) means that the religion of the citizens is dictated by the ruler. With a sacral society, if the leader changed religion, so did the country. Examples of sacral enforcement can be seen in Europe's history of wars in the Middle Ages, or in the demand for uniformity of faith in nations today. The United States Constitution attempted to break the sacral pattern by not establishing a national religion, thereby protecting citizens' personal choices of faith.

A sacral society cannot tolerate dissenters. Who stood out as non-conformists in early Rome and beyond? Jews! Ever since

Constantine, Jewish communities have been forced either to convert to the national faith, be exiled, or killed. Many Christian dissenters also paid for their lack of conformity by being burned at the stake.

Redefinition of "the Church"

Redefining the nature of the church was the second great damage done by Constantine's pattern. To be "Christian" was simply to be born into the Roman Empire. This meant that the Church embraced the masses, regardless of whether they were genuinely converted or not. To see the difference between sacral adherence and individual choice, compare an *"ecclesia"* made up of those who choose to follow Jesus with a "Church" consisting of everyone born into a nation. Of course, membership numbers would be vastly different, since newborns were enrolled by christening. The act of baptism was changed from an active statement of faith to a passive act done to a child. This foundational dichotomy remains in Christian churches today.

Constantine's Coercive Use of the Sword

The third way Constantine altered Christianity was to arm the church with the sword. One of the Savior's beatitudes was "blessed are the peace makers" (Matthew 5:9a). How antithetical it was for those entrusted with representing the Prince of peace to wield the sword! Willam J. Ouweneel, in *The Eternal People,* quotes from a French novel titled *The Last of the Just,* by A. Schwarz-Bart. In it, Ernie Levy says this about Christians to his fiancée Golda:

> I've been to their churches and I've read their gospel. Do you know who the Christ was? A simple Jew like your father. A kind of Hassid. . . . [H]e was a really good Jew, you know, sort of like the Baal Shem Tov—a merciful man, and gentle. The Christians say they love him, but I think they hate him without knowing it. So they

> take the cross by the other end and make a sword out of
> it and strike us with it! . . . Poor Jesus, if he came back
> to earth and saw that the pagans had made a sword out
> of him and used it against his sisters and brothers, he'd
> be sad, he'd grieve forever. (106)

Well grasped, poignantly stated.

To repeat, Constantine's "in this sign conquer" sent a bowling ball down history leaving a tragic trail of forced "conversions," bloody crusades, and recurrent wars between "Christian" nations in the name of sacral (theocratic) conformity. The peaceable ambassadors of Christ's Kingdom of God were overridden by a man-made Christen-dom with its added suffix "dom"—for "dominion"—i.e., rule.

However, there were always dissenters who refused to cooperate with the Church's weaponization. They were persecuted and derided, called by the derogatory term "staff carriers" (rather than "sword carriers"). Leonard Verduin's chapter on this problem in *The Reformers and Their Stepchildren* documents the struggle of these "heretics" who resisted coercion.

Both Faith Communities' "Wanderings"

The Scriptures describe Israel's early "wilderness wanderings," and history reveals their ongoing wanderings over the earth. Likewise, very early in history, Christianity began wandering in its own wilderness. Jews took the brunt of Christendom's misguided paths, and Christian dissenters were also deeply impacted. Meanwhile, divergent theological interpretations arose. Their seriously differing mindsets need to be considered next.

7

What undergirded Christendom's interpretation that the Church had replaced Israel?

Two men are central in the developing transformation: Constantine (AD 272–337) and Augustine (AD 354–430). While Constantine's influence was political and geographical, it was Augustine whose teaching led to a trend in theological interpretation.

Although there is much to admire in Augustine, we need to investigate one damaging area of his ongoing influence, the church's method of scriptural interpretation (hermeneutics). It is only fair to start by placing him in the historical setting of his times. His best-known works are *The Confessions of St. Augustine,* and *The City of God.* The deduction that Israel had been replaced by the Church had grown out of historical circumstances. Rome had taken Jerusalem and destroyed the Jewish Temple in AD 70, and whoever was left of the Jews had to scatter. Two years later had come the tragedy of a thousand Jews taking their lives at the Masada fortress, rather than being slaughtered by the Romans. It would have been natural for Rome to conclude that they had permanently finished Israel and Judaism.

Gentiles Started to Outnumber the Jewish Believers

Remember that the first five thousand believers in Jesus after his Resurrection were Jewish (see Acts chapters 1–5). Soon after Steven's stoning, great persecution broke out against the fledgling church, scattering many. Jewish businesspeople were already living in Rome, and some Jews scattered by persecution became refugees there too. Nero and later emperors continued to pour out persecution on Jews, whether or not they were Christians. Nevertheless, believers in the Lord Jesus Christ were multiplying across the Empire. Chapter 6 focused on the influence of Constantine. Even many of his troops were Christians when this would-be emperor had his vision of the cross with its message, "in this sign conquer." Constantine may have thought that Rome's Gentile Christians would carry his rule, plus Christianity, forward. Not being a student of the Word, based on his questionable vision, he introduced both sacralism and the sword as tools for multiplying the ranks of the faith.

Dismissal of the Formerly Jewish Landmarks

Furthermore, it is significant that Constantine's mother, Helena, took great interest in the Holy Land. She set about having Christian churches built in Jerusalem, ignoring history, and relocating structures away from geographical places long revered in Israel's past. A fifth-century mosaic discovered in 1884 on the floor of a church in present-day Jordan is called the "Madaba Map" of Jerusalem. It demonstrates how Christendom's pilgrims and the mosaic artist who created the Madaba map viewed Jerusalem by the 400s AD.

> This map has a strong political direction following the policies of the emperor Constantine. Most telling is the absence of any Jewish landmark. The Temple Mount has been expunged and is indicated by a single black line of stones, although steps leading up from the Pool

of Siloam can be easily identified. (*Bible Versus Tradition,* 18)

Neither the Temple Mount nor the City of David are included on the map, having lost their significance for the Byzantines. This map's discovery confirms archeologists' questions about the authenticity of where Christian churches were constructed and named in the early centuries, evidently ignoring, or replacing, original Jewish structures.

Supersessionism's Theological Buttressing

The Church's disposal of all things Jewish was expressed geographically, but it was accompanied by theological buttressing as well. To trace the development of supersessionism, we need to go back to Christendom's most influential church father, Saint Augustine, who followed soon after Constantine. Informed by Platonic and Socratic philosophy, he is known as probably the greatest Christian philosopher of antiquity, and surely the one with the most lasting influence. Saint Augustine's metaphorical interpretation of Scripture deeply influenced both Catholic and Reformed doctrine and practice. Scriptures can have various levels of meaning. The metaphorical interpretation of the Bible tends to focus on the perceived spiritual sense rather than the literal sense. For example, the Song of Solomon has been interpreted allegorically to be referring to the love Christ has for the Church. Notice the Gentile-ized Christ and the Church being substituted for Jewish King Solomon and his beloved. Such reinterpretations demonstrate the danger of de-historicization. Taking the original passage out of its historical context can give license to mishandling the text of Scripture.

There is a difference between interpreting passages in their historical context versus allegorical interpretations of the biblical narrative. The metaphorical view tends to read backward from Christ to the Old Testament, rather than the reverse. These two handlings of basic aspects of God's Word have set up long-standing divisions between Christians. Although metaphorical gleanings can yield rich personal applications, their alteration of meanings as they were written becomes especially evident as applied to past history or future promises. For instance, the tribes of Israel are focal in Revelation 7 and 14, and Jerusalem is the center of Revelation 22. The metaphorical method of interpretation reasons, "If the Jews are finished, how can we deal with the Jewish foundations in the Old Testament Scriptures? What shall we do with God's restorative promises to his chosen people? What will we do with all the Jewish references in Revelation? We can't take them to mean literally what they say. Since the Jews are finished, they can't really be for Israel. Our solution could be to declare them to be metaphorical. We have replaced Israel, so all those references and promises really should be applied to the Church."

Opposite Presuppositions

So, one segment of Christendom assumes that the biblical promises now belong to the Church. Another segment believes that God's promises to his chosen people remain theirs. These two presuppositions lead to two very different ways of thinking and to different expectations. The disparity even affects both groups' willingness to stay in fellowship with each other.

The variations noticeably surface when discussing prophetic passages. Prophecy is a special category of Scripture, one function of which is to prove authenticity. The Bible speaks often about false and true prophets. A prophet's authenticity was to be tested by whether what was prophesied actually came true (see Deuteronomy 18:22). Example after example of this testing is on display in the Bible. The most striking case was that of the ultimate prophet, Jesus, predicting the actuality and timing of his death and resurrection, followed by their exact fulfillments.

A major problem arises today from opposite interpretations of what is prophesied for Israel's future. While some consider Israel finished and stripped of her uniqueness, others honor God's eternal love for the family he chose to bring forth the Patriarchs, the Scriptures, the Messiah, and the rich legacy that Gentile believers now enjoy. This issue is Christendom's little-discussed "elephant in the room." The dichotomy has deeply affected how Jews have been treated all down through the centuries. Although often unrecognized, it lies beneath attitudes and actions toward the nation of Israel and her citizens still today. Antisemitism is currently on the rise in the Holocaust's Europe and even in America, despite the sacrifice of soldiers who died fighting against Nazism in World War II.

Christendom's Need to Acknowledge and Repent

A powerful call to the Church to repent is Barry E. Horner's *Future Israel: Why Christian Anti-Judaism Must Be Challenged.* It chronicles the Church's history of anti-Judaism over the centuries, partially based on Augustinian eschatology.

Another plea that documents the Church's unscriptural treatment of Jews is Marvin R. Wilson's *Our Father Abraham: Jewish Roots of the Christian Faith.* On the back cover, Carl E. Armerding of Regent College in Vancouver, British Columbia, summarized the book's thesis this way: "Wilson has thrown down a theological gauntlet, challenging Christians of all kinds to reform a two-thousand-year-old history of misunderstanding Jews and misinterpreting our own sources." In the book's chapter on "A History of Contempt: Antisemitism and the Church," Marvin Wilson documents Gentile attitudes toward Jews that developed in the early centuries. Christian clerics often cite Augustine with total admiration. Wilson sees Augustine's allegorical interpretation of the Bible as an attempt to deal with the Jewish-related Scriptures. Since the early Gentile church fathers assumed they had replaced Israel, it was as if the Church had become adversary to the parent that had given it birth.

Wilson quotes Richard Longenecker's *New Testament Social Ethics* as saying, "For the Church, therefore, to admit any real connection with the Old Testament as a propaedeutic to the gospel would be to grant a measure of legitimacy and historical validity to the Jewish people" (96). This caught the Church in a bind. How could the Old Testament that buttressed the Messianic claims of Jesus be done away with? Augustine's solution was allegory. This is Marvin Wilson's assessment:

> In allegory, the Old Testament could be made a "Christian" document. Through their efforts to spiritualize, typologize, and christologize the text, the early Church Fathers were able to find abundant Christian meaning in the Old Testament. Christ, or New Testament thought, was *read into*, rather than *out of*, the biblical text in some of the most obscure places. Accordingly, Irenaeus, Origen, Augustine, and others developed a system of allegorical exegesis that had the disastrous effect of wrenching the biblical text from its plain historical meaning. (97)

He concludes that allegorical interpretations are both suspect and risky, having abandoned the plain meaning of the words in the context of their specific historical and cultural setting. They lead to a wasteland of subjectivity. To quote Bible teacher Alistair Begg's exegetical warning, "Remember that the main things are the plain things, and the plain things are the main things."

Fresh Considerations in the Scholarly World

Recent biblical scholars are pursuing an historical rather than the former theological mode of interpretation. Rabbi Mark S. Kinzer's *Jerusalem Crucified, Jerusalem Risen* pleads for re-thinking Christendom's traditional false doctrines which he summarizes in this way:

> The Torah has been abolished, the Jewish people are under divine wrath, the eschatological inheritance

consists of heaven or a glorified universe (with no eschatological significance attached to the land of Israel), and the *euangelion* concerns the eternal destiny of individuals (or the *ekklesia*) and has nothing to do with the national identity of the people. (275)

Rabbi Kinzer points out "That fracturing of the *euangelion* meant that through much of the past two thousand years it has been impossible for Jews to respond to the entire prophetic message of the resurrected Messiah by entering the *ekklesia*" (287).

Getting the Big Story Wrong

Gerald R. McDermott, Anglican Chair of Divinity at Beeson Divinity School, has gathered ten writers' fresh perspectives on Israel and the land in a book titled *The New Christian Zionism*. They explore Zionism's Old and New Testament roots established long before the rise of nineteenth-century Zionism. The book opens with an historically helpful and currently challenging chapter titled "A History of Superssionism: Getting the Big Story Wrong." Contributors explore this underlying inaccuracy in pre-conceived biblical theology, its historical outworking, and its prophetical implications for the future. This scholarly recalculation is extremely important, for it is in theological institutions that error is perpetuated and passed on to the laity.

Practical Repercussion

Lay people in churches tend to trust whatever their respected theologians teach. It is a rare church member who studies the whole Word of God carefully and is therefore enabled to discern error. Dissent is rarely encouraged. Metaphorically based theology, when too broadly applied, tends to create alternative meanings of Scripture. This methodology may also have played a role in the Church's habit of inventing extra-biblical traditions. These practices have powerfully impacted the lives of adherents, the focus of our next exploration.

8

What abuses developed when Church traditions superseded the Word of God?

Along with the Church's departure from biblical truth related to the LORD's chosen people, other nonbiblical substitutions began to emerge. The Hebrew calendar based on the moon was changed to a Gregorian calendar based on the sun. The seven biblical feasts of the Hebrews were forbidden, and a new Christian calendar devised. The center of worship changed from home churches to cathedrals. Apostolic leadership morphed into the Papacy. The High Priest's garments reappeared in elaborate vestments of the clergy. Christening was substituted for baptism, the Mass for the Lord's supper. Were these man-made traditions created by and for Gentile Christianity? How in tune with the teachings of Jesus do these substitutions appear to be?

Jesus' "Woes" on Religious Leadership

When we look at *Yeshua*'s life, we hear both compassion and denunciation. His compassion for prostitutes and tax collectors offended the Scribes and Pharisees. Significantly, the Lord's most scorching condemnation fell on religious leadership. Matthew 23 records Jesus' "woes" on the priesthood of his generation:

> Woe to you, teachers of the law and Pharisees, you
> hypocrites. You shut the kingdom of heaven in men's
> faces. . . . Woe to you, blind guides . . . You are like
> whitewashed tombs . . . You brood of vipers . . . (see
> Matthew 23:13–36 for Jesus' woes)

> Oh Jerusalem, Jerusalem, you who kill the prophets
> and stone those sent to you, how often I have longed
> to gather your children together, as a hen gathers her
> chicks under her wings, but you were not willing. (see
> Matthew 23:37–39 for his grief)

This rebuke stood as a warning to religious leadership then, and
also cautions those of us who represent religion now.

No Man-Invented Program

Beyond the activity of the Holy Spirit, how elaborately did the
Savior provide for his followers' future organization? What
practices for believers did the Lord set up? Before his impending departure, his only mention of formal procedures were
baptism and times of remembering his broken body and shed
blood (see Matthew 28:19; Luke 22:9; 1 Corinthians 11:23–26).
His followers had little organization other than being drawn
together by their love for Him. He left no human successor in
charge, but promised them his divine replacement, the Holy
Spirit. He outlined no program, but expected the Spirit of God
to direct the next steps in the process of announcing the offer
of redemption to the whole world. The disciples were only told
to go out and give witness to what they had seen and heard. The
Spirit was promised to be their counselor and power.

> When the Counselor comes, whom I will send to you
> from the Father, the Spirit of truth who goes out from
> the Father, he will testify about me. And you also must
> testify, for you have been with me from the beginning.
> (John 15:26–27)

Just before the Lord's ascension into heaven forty days after his Resurrection, his disciples were still focused on a political victory. They asked, "Lord, are you at this time going to restore the kingdom to Israel?" His answer:

> It is not for you to know the times and dates the Father has set by his own authority, but you will receive power when the Holy Spirit comes on you, and you will be my witnesses in Jerusalem, and all Judea and Samaria, and to the ends of the earth. (Acts 1:7–8)

Holy Spirit Empowered Continuation

The book of Acts describes that promised outpouring of the Holy Spirit ten days later when Jews from abroad gathered in Jerusalem for the Feast of Weeks, what we now call Pentecost (see Acts 2). Suddenly, the Spirit transformed fearful Peter to bravely give testimony. Due to the glorification of Jesus in heaven (see Acts 2:33), this outpouring launched the disciples into a far-reaching series of Spirit-empowered testimonies to the resurrected Messiah's authenticity and dominion.

The good news spread quickly across the Near East and into Macedonia and Greece. Clusters of believers met in homes. Elders were charged to guard their flocks. The Gospel was so transforming that the faith was spreading unceremoniously from person to person.

Non-Biblical Traditions Multiplying

In contrast to the Lord's simple dedication to God's Word and expectation of the Spirit, over the centuries Christendom's leadership added a succession of doctrines and traditions that bound constituents firmly to the power and authority of the clergy—priests presumed to be intercessors, veneration of saints, transubstantiation of the Mass, Mary as a co-Redemptrix, and Papal infallibility, to name a few. Crusades, Inquisitions, and religious wars overrode God's Gospel of the Prince of peace. The authority and sufficiency of Scripture were being left behind. These infamous abuses are well documented and need to be admitted.

Meanwhile dissenters from these abuses realized that the Church was wandering from its source. When they protested, they were disciplined by excommunication, banishment, or execution. The extent of religious manipulation became more and more obvious with the introduction of payments to the Church called "indulgences"—supposedly to help departed loved ones get out of an invented "purgatory." These are some of the ugly barnacles that accumulated over the centuries on the ship called Christendom.

"Scapegoat" Victimization of Jews

Since the Temple and its sacrifices were gone, a rabbinical Judaism developed to hold Jewish communities together. But in country after country all Jewish descendants were often held responsible for "Christ killing," even though the Lord of the Church had absolved his Jewish and Roman crucifiers when he cried from the cross, "Father, forgive them, for they do not know what they are doing" (Luke 23:34). Each generation of Jews was blamed for plagues and other societal catastrophes. During the Middle Ages this resulted in terrible successions of abuses, disenfranchisements, forced conversions, ghettos, mass exiles, and executions of Jews. The record of the world's persecution of this one community throughout history has been so diabolical that the hatred expressed can only be traced to God's arch enemy, Satan. In the Bible Satan is called "the prince of this world" (see John 12:31, 14:30).

Then came Martin Luther. In the badly needed reformation of the Church, this passionate man played a powerful role—but also a Jewish-related regrettable role in the annals of the Church, the subject of our next consideration.

9

Why did the Reformation address three key problems, but fail regarding Jews?

Throughout the Roman Catholic Church's domination over centuries, some who studied the Bible realized how far afield the Church was leading its adherents. Dissenters who raised their heads were summarily silenced, branded as heretics, and sometimes were drowned or burned at the stake. These facts are documented in Leonard Verduin's book, *The Reformers and their Stepchildren*. The groundswell of dissent came to a head in the person of Martin Luther in 1517. His Ninety-five Theses nailed to the Wittenberg Church door led to a convergence of resistance that we call the Reformation—a complicated study in itself.

Incomplete Reformation

The Reformation brought forth three doctrinal affirmations known as "*sola Scriptura, sola gratia, and sola fide*,"—Latin for "scripture alone, grace alone, and faith alone." In other words, it affirmed that biblical Christian faith is based solely on the Scriptures, salvation is only by grace, and redemption is not obtained by works but only by faith. Luther did not mean to leave the Church, but his fellow reformers came to be generally known as protesters—later called "Protestants"—although what they protested varied widely. Some groups meant just to reform Catholicism. "Heretics" known as "anabaptists" (second baptizers, although christened at birth) believed that scripturally, baptism should accompany profession of faith. When the Reformation did not deal with Church-conferred membership by infant baptism, the anabaptists broke off entirely.

What does the Reformation have to do with our Jew/Gentile relational problem? Yes, Luther's call back to the Scriptures served to immensely strengthen believers. However, some Scriptures seemed to be overlooked, especially the biblical guidelines about Jewish and Gentile relationships, and God's prophetic promises to Israel.

Luther's Lethal Legacy

Unfortunately, although he is known as hero to the Christian world, and earlier was friendly to Jews, in his later life Luther's attitude toward Germany's Jews turned fatally flawed. So vitriolic were Luther's quotations, that they served to numb the resistance of the German church to Hitler's Nazi doctrine of Aryan supremacy. The legacy of Christendom's unbiblical stance toward Jews probably undergirded Christian Europe's failure to stand against Hitler's "final solution."

Even after the Nazi horrors, America seems to have forgotten Jewish vulnerability. Harkening back to *Bonhoeffer*, his 2010 study of Dietrich Bonhoeffer's life, Eric Metaxas' 2022 *Letter to the American Church* includes a chapter named "The Church and the Jewish Question." He points out to American leadership Hitler's recruitment of the German Church:

> Jesus was Himself a Jew, as were each of the twelve disciples and most in the early Church. That the Nazi government would suddenly wipe away two millennia with one stroke and determine that the German Church must be organized along racial and antisemitic lines was perfect madness and obviously untenable. But what's amazing and horrifying is that many in the

German Church—like many in the American Church now—were willing to look the other way, even on something that touched the very fundamentals of the faith in which they professed to believe. They wished to get along and not be seen as "troublemakers." (38–39)

The Foundational Error Too Threatening to Admit

The Holocaust's roots went back further than the 1930s, way back to the Gentiles' basic concept that the Church had replaced Israel, back to Constantine and throughout the Middle Ages. Therefore, at the time of the Reformation, to recognize that Christendom's treatment of Jews had been wrong would have been to admit its very foundation was flawed. It would threaten Christendom's long-held unscriptural and therefore inauthentic assumption. What might such an admission mean to the power structures of the Church? The consequences would be threatening and unthinkable! Furthermore, expectations for Israel's future in God's plan did not make sense, since at that time there were no indications of promises to Israel actually coming to light. The Church simply assumed that God's promises to the Old Testament people of God were now awarded to the Church. Only the curses remained for Israel.

Supersessionism's long-assumed mentality was ingrained enough to pass on down from Catholicism to Protestantism unchallenged in the sixteenth century and continues to be endemic to most faith communities yet today.

It would take the horror of the Holocaust to shock the guilty Church into admitting the need for a place for Jews to simply *be*. The Holocaust led to questioning the bitter fruit of the Church's assumptions. A revealing case where race overrode faith was the sentencing of a Jewish nun named Edith Stein who was disposed of at Auschwitz, Christian though she was. Her story and the facts of history disillusioned a former Catholic priest, James Carroll, as told in his piercing book and

DVD, *Constantine's Sword*. As reflected in another book's title, *Israel, My Chosen People: A German Confession Before God and the Jews*, M. Basilea Schlink poignantly grieved over Hitler Germany's horrible guilt. She also called for recognizing a wider and deeper guilt—man's profound hatred of God.

The Holocaust of the 1940s resulted in the highly resisted regathering of the Jewish people in their homeland in 1948. It took the resurgence of Israel—her "bones" reconnecting, her regathering, her nation being "born in a day"—to signal to the Vatican the possibility of having followed a misguided path. But would Christendom be willing to rethink its whole history? If not, Israel would continue to be declared illegitimate. This remains the unquestioned verdict of much of Christendom yet today.

Was reticence to help Jews only a European and Middle Eastern problem? What about the United States? Strangely, Jews were barred from largescale immigration as they tried to flee from Europe in the 1920s. Eventually, however, the largest population of Jews outside of Israel did immigrate to America. Nevertheless, doctrinal anti-Judaism/Semitism continued to be implicitly assumed—although largely unrecognized—in Catholic, Anglican, Lutheran, and many mainline Protestant churches.

Surprising Rise of the Messianic Jewish Movement

A few decades ago, an unexpected thing occurred: the emergence of Jewish believers in Jesus as God's true Messiah. Since the 1970s the Messianic Jewish movement has continued to multiply in Israel and the USA. A 2023 film called "The Jesus Revolution" replays the amazing renewal movement that swept over California's hippie community in 1972, some of whom happened to be Jewish. They eventually found each other and started Jewish congregations in the United States. Meanwhile a stirring was rising in Israel, as unveiled in David H. Sterns surprising publications in 1988, one for the believing Jewish community: *Messianic Jewish Manifesto*, and another to awaken Gentiles: *Restoring the Jewishness of the Gospel*.

Today, around the world, including in Israel, there are hundreds of Jewish congregations who do trust and worship *Yeshua* as the world's Messiah. A transformation is taking place as the "olive tree" is beginning to bud again. Jewish believers are proclaiming *Yeshua's* Messiahship. The inseparability of the two Covenants is being increasingly demonstrated by recently published writings, even including Messianic Bible translations such as Stern's *The Complete Jewish Bible* and the Messianic Jewish Family Bible Project's *Tree of Life Bible*.

This unprecedented phenomenon produces a potential bridge between Jews and Christians. An insightful voice from that bridging community came from Jonathan Bernis, a Messianic Jewish Christian leader. At a Promise Keepers convention focused on racial reconciliation, Jonathan Bernis represented Jews among predominantly black and white Gentile Christian men as they sought to humbly affirm their unity in Christ. The premise of Bernis' "Roadblocks to Redemption" article in Jewish Voice Today (mentioned in chapter 6) helps Christians to realize that replacement theology shut the door of faith to the Jewish community, even though *Yeshua* was and is the most Jewish of all Jews.

Re-Evaluation Now Growing

Nevertheless, replacement theology's assumption that the Church is the "new Israel" has such deep roots that it is explicitly and implicitly taught. Its falseness is slowly being uncovered and confessed by a small minority of Gentile believers. Israel's firm place in God's purposes is being re-considered by thoughtful Christian scholars.

Already mentioned in chapter 2 was Marvin Wilson's ground-breaking book published in 1987 titled *Our Father*

Abraham: Jewish Roots of the Christian Faith. Wilson was a leading scholar on Christian/Jewish relations and a professor of Biblical and Theological Studies at Gordon College. Rabbi A. James Rudin's endorsement of this book says, "His superb scholarship is combined with many concrete suggestions for building new relationships between the church and the synagogue, between Christians and Jews." In his forward, Wilson explains:

> Although this work is a biblical, historical, and cultural study, the reader will quickly find out that it is concerned with more than exploring the past. Learning to think Hebraically is only the start. These pages also have a contemporary application: they are a call for Christians to reexamine their Jewish roots so as to affect a more authentically biblical lifestyle. (xvi) . . . It focuses on Christian-Jewish relations throughout two thousand years of history. Here we trace the Jewish beginnings of the Church and the various actors which led to its split from the Synagogue. We also trace the history of contempt between Church and Synagogue, showing how the de-Judaization of the Church led to anti-Judaism and antisemitism. (xvii)

Since Israel has become a nation again, biblically informed believers are trying to awaken Christians to come to terms with the spoiled relationship with Jews. Based on talks given to a Jewish community years before are Markus Barth's statements in *Israel and the Church,* published in 1969 and again in 2005. Following are two of his pleas.

On Christians' wrong attitudes:

> Too often it was seen as the Christians' duty to preach "at" the Jews, to denounce and scold them. No respect, no reverence, was shown; no mention made of what we owe them; no acknowledgement given of our dreadful guilt against them. After all the subtle and grievous wrong that in the name of Christ and of the church

has been done to the Jews throughout the centuries, the first thing to be done now certainly is not an act of condescension or so-called generosity on the part of us Christians. . . . What we ought to beg from the Jews is forgiveness—forgiveness of the same kind as the prodigal will have to ask from his older brother if ever these two brothers are to live together in the father's household. (114)

On peace accomplished by Christ (see Ephesians 2:16–18, 3:5–6, 4:14–18):

The manifold tensions between Christians and Jews—some openly admitted, some hidden or repressed—cannot obliterate the peace brought by Jesus the Messiah. The Messianic peace is a reality despite human incomprehension, denial, rebellion against it. . . . this peace that was made and proclaimed by Christ is not to be undone. Some misled soldiers may continue warring long after the conclusion of peace. They deprive themselves and others of the fruits of peace. Yet the peace already concluded is real and valid. . . . Brotherhood with Israel is therefore in Ephesians not just a possible or desirable consequence of the eternal plan of God, of the making of peace through the cross of Christ, and of the revelation of his mystery through the Spirit. What God has planned, performed, and revealed has no other content and character than precisely this full community of the Gentiles with Israel. (91–92)

Another powerful resource is *Future Israel: Why Christian Anti-Judaism Must Be Challenged*, published in 2007, mentioned in chapter 7. The author is Barry Horner, whose degrees are from Westminster Theological Seminary and Western Conservative Baptist Theological Seminary. His last chapter draws this haunting conclusion:

Here we are not dealing with an eschatological refinement concerning which we can agree to disagree. If the Christian Church in general over the centuries had followed Paul's exhortation in Romans 11:17–24, 31, it is not unreasonable to conceive that the tragic treatment of the Jews during the twentieth century that resulted in the ashes of nearly a whole nation might have been replaced with the fruit of a great harvest of Jewish souls saved because they had been lovingly provoked to jealousy (Romans 11:11), to the glory of God (Romans 11:36). (330)

Opposite Conclusions

In the minds of a remnant of Gentile Christians today, this flowering of biblical Jewish faith in *Yeshua* authenticates God's promises to his chosen people. It suggests the nearing conclusion of the "age of the Gentiles" (see Romans 11:25–26). It could be seen as a harbinger of the ultimate High Priest *Yeshua's* eventual return (see Hebrews 9:24, 28). But to many, the emergence of Messianic Jewish Christians is an embarrassing anomaly at best, and potentially a catastrophic blow to the Church's replacement doctrine and accompanying practices formerly thought to be unquestionably firm.

10

What legacies from the past alienate Jews and Gentiles (the nations) today?

Looking back at how Christendom veered away from the Scriptures, and the Reformation's failure to deal with its "replacement" stance, we find Jewish and Gentile relationships still deeply affected by the past. Not only in Christendom, but world-wide attitudes are registered and politicized by the actions and condemnations of the United Nations. According to Noa Tishby's book, *Israel: A Simple Guide to the Most Misunderstood Country on Earth*, Israel is the UN's favorite target, with more resolutions against Israel than Iran, Syria, North Korea, and Russia combined. She provides statistics in a chapter titled, "What's with the obsession, world?"

Denominational Variances

Christian denominations in America find themselves deeply divided on Israel's situation today. Jerusalem continues to be, as Scripture predicts, "a cup of reeling" (see Zechariah 12:2). What is behind these divisions? The Roman Church has an unfortunate history with antisemitism from its beginnings, and especially Italy and the Vatican's relationship to the Holocaust. How about Protestants? In the New World, the American experiment broke the hold of Europe's sacralism (church/state union), allowing individual choice of faith to be practiced. Naturally that freedom led to denominationalism, often related to the languages and cultures from which various communities came to the New World.

In the last few decades, some churches have changed their names and distanced their commitments to former doctrinal origins. Churchgoers form their theologies rather implicitly from Catholic, Reformed, Anabaptist, or Pentecostal, etc. mentors or a mixture. We tend to trust the theology passed down by our families, pastors, and teachers. But when churchgoers melt together, they find their different doctrinal suppositions to be puzzling.

Israel a Flashpoint of Division

It follows that a sore point of conflict can surface when Israel is the subject. The world's confused situation today leads people to think about what the "end times" may mean, and how Israel fits into God's purposes. Whether prophetic passages referring to Israel are taken to be actual or metaphorical is an underlying issue that leads to differing viewpoints.

Looking at the wider situation, how is Christendom faring today? Christianity languishes in Europe. Cathedrals are often more like museums than overflowing with worshippers. Faith is eroding in secular America, the one nation whose unique foundation was theoretically Judeo/Christian. Laws restricting public prayer and the once-honored Ten Commandments have been put in place. Commitment to scriptural teaching is eroding even in many churches today.

Only a remnant of Christians now affirms God's continuing love for his chosen people, and honors those from whom came the Patriarchs, our Bible, our Savior, and the Christ for whom Christians are named. Not only religious divisions, but also political divides are seen in our contemporary Christian world. What religious doctrine leads to what political attitude?

If Israel were deemed cancelled and the Gentile church having now taken over, then the Scripture's prophecies related to Israel and Jerusalem must be declared to be either "in the past" (called Preterism) or else transferred to Christendom (Supersessionism). If all things Jewish are dismissed, then Israel would be seen as only one nation among many, with no biblical claim to the Holy Land. Her scriptural legacy would therefore be dismissed, nullified, denied, even vilified, and resisted in philosophical and political ways. An Israel-delegitimizing response is seen in one Christian group's BDS movement (Boycott, Divest, Sanction) dedicated to opposing Israel today.

The Current Palestinian Tragedy

Of course, reasonable sympathy for the Palestinian struggle further complicates the Middle East situation. Outsiders ponder the confusing claims, and the UN exerts its own bias. *The War of Return* by Adi Schwartz and Einat Wilf, is a 2020 study that denigrates the UNRWA (United Nations Relief and Works Agency for Palestinian Refugees in the Near East) as actually obstructing peace.

Jealousy of the "chosen sons" within Abraham's ancient family still smolders. Aggressions and retaliations are not forgotten. Centuries later, what to do with surviving Jews in light of the Holocaust was a conundrum that resulted in what Palestinians experience as a catastrophe. It seems that ruthless partisan managers relentlessly use ancient hurts to fan flames of resentment and hatred, even though the resulting fallouts destroy their own communities.

To get a feel for opposite viewpoints about this impasse, compare two Christian Palestinians' passionate accounts: Mitri Raheb's vantage point in *Faith in the Face of Empire* with Tass Saada's *The Mind of Terror*. These two Palestinians see the contemporary situation quite differently.

For a unique Palestinian/Israeli encounter with both communities, consider the amazing saga previously mentioned, *Son of Hamas,* by the Palestinian named Mosab Hassan Yousef. For an immersion into Israel's struggle, read Jewish writer Yossi Klein Halevi's *Letters to My Palestinian Neighbor.* He tries to let his neighbor feel the pain of being lied about. "The relentless message from the Palestinian media is that there was no ancient Temple in Jerusalem, no Jewish attachment to the Western Wall, no archaeological proof of Jewish roots in the land at all" (141).

Many sources have reported huge truckloads of excavations recently dug out from under the Temple Mount and dumped as trash. Archeologists were appalled at this treatment of ancient and sacred Jewish artifacts. Halevi even raises the question of who really owns the Holy Land. From God's agricultural commandments in Leviticus, Halevi concludes:

> The message is that a holy land doesn't belong to us but to God. The elusiveness of possession is an expression of the land's holiness. The sacred can never be fully owned by mortal beings. Sacred space is an encounter with a world beyond boundaries, a dimension in which all human claims are irrelevant. . . . For me the very conditionality of ownership, the fact that no one and no people can really own holy land, offers a religious basis for sharing the land between us. As custodians, not owners. (148)

In Leviticus 25:23 the LORD said, "The land must not be sold permanently, because the land is mine and you are but aliens and my tenants."

The Perpetual Jewish Tragedy

After they were scattered out of the land, Israelites suffered a long history of being starved, killed, or exiled. Jewish homes, lives, and fortunes were stolen in country after country. Most Gentiles today are unaware of these horrific abuses. (Detailed documentation is available in a book noted in chapter 2, Edward

H. Flannery's *The Anguish of the Jews: Twenty-Three Centuries of Antisemitism.)* Furthermore, escapees were denied entrance as refugees by nation after nation, including the United States, when Jews were fleeing the Nazi's calculated program of extermination. The very fact that God's chosen people have survived up to today is a miracle that we can only attribute to him.

In 2010, the prize-winning British journalist Melanie Phillips released a huge volume titled *The World Turned Upside Down.* In chapter 17, "The Revival of Christian Jew-Hatred," she documents this ongoing manifestation, points to supersessionism as its root, and asserts that a Jewish homeland has failed to redeem Christian guilt for the Holocaust.

Challenges to Our Generation of Christians and Jews

But regarding Christendom's need to grapple with past and present Jew/Gentile religious alienation, new voices are calling us to rethink complications arising out of former presuppositions.

A thoughtful resource already noted comes from Barry E. Horner's *Future Israel: Why Christian Anti-Judaism Must Be Challenged.* One of Horner's appendices makes available a sixteen-page annotated bibliography of "Christ and Jewish Relations in Church History." Another appendix prints Melanie Phillip's essay on Replacement Theology. The bibliography's brief overviews of thirty-five authors' books on these subjects provide a valuable resource for the motivated searcher.

Meanwhile, how is this impasse being played out in the various Jewish communities? Although influential, Orthodox Jews are a minority in Israel. Secular Jews (the majority in Israel and America today) without a Torah-directed faith cannot appeal to the Scriptures for Israel's authentic claim to her homeland. The small but growing community of Messianic Jews who do believe in Jesus are resisted by both Orthodox and secular Israelis.

How does the confusing Jewish/Christian divide manifest itself among Christians? Many either don't know or don't trust these Jewish people who call themselves "Messianic Jews." Since Judaism and Christianity have been seen as separate and opposing for centuries, the idea of "Jews for Jesus" not only offends Jews but also seems suspect to many Christians.

Reviewing How This Generation of Jewish Believers in *Yeshua* Chose to be Called

It would help Christians to understand this new manifestation by learning how the term "Messianic Jews" came to be the designation for Jesus-believing Jews. As already explained in chapter 1, Paul Liberman, a Jewish lawyer, recounted how their designation as "Messianic Jews" was chosen. His book has a strange title for a believer in Jesus: *Don't Call Me Christian.* Reviewing the background story: An unexpected moving of the Spirit among hippies in the 1970s in California created what came to be called "the Jesus people." Some among them were Jewish. At first each thought themselves a sole Jewish believer in *Yeshua.* Eventually they found each other, grouped together, and matured.

In former days, Jewish Christians had been a tiny minority, and were called "Hebrew Christians." They had simply assimilated into churches. In contrast, these hippie-background Christians found that most church people didn't welcome them, and Christians did not seem committed to reaching Jewish people with the Gospel of *Yeshua.* They wondered what they should call themselves. Considering Christendom's relentless persecution of Jews, and Christian Europe's cooperation with the Holocaust, the Jewish community would instinctively be repelled by all things labeled "Christian." *Don't Call me Christian* unpacks for the reader the new Jewish community's inhouse battle over what to call themselves. Those eager to reach their community pointed out that if they used the old term "Hebrew

Christians" or chose the name "Christian Jews" it would shut the door of witness to their own people. Finally, they chose the term "Messianic Jews," a title that honored *Yeshua* as the Messiah and yet remained Jewish.

Encouraging and Discouraging Signs

That decision seems to have been helpful, for the Messianic movement has multiplied amazingly. By now hundreds of Messianic congregations in the USA and over the world worship Jesus as the Messiah. Many are in Tel Aviv, Jerusalem, and throughout Israel. For lists of congregations in the United States and Israel, see any issue of *Messianic Times*, a bi-monthly magazine serving the international Messianic Jewish community. For over thirty years, Messiah College in Pennsylvania has hosted the annual conference of the Messianic Jewish Alliance in America, one of the larger such associations. Over a thousand American and Israeli believers in Jesus usually attend this very Jewish week-long convention.

Their claim to be better Jews after receiving Jesus as the Messiah sounds strange to most Jewish ears. Jakob Jocz writes in *The Jewish People and Jesus Christ after Auschwitz:* "Many of the young Jews in the Jews for Jesus movement were estranged from Jewish tradition and even hostile to it. They recovered their Jewishness as a result of their conversion" (213).

In a collection of fourteen authors' chapters in a book titled *Unity: Awakening the One New Man*, Dr. Craig Keener points out the unique role of Messianic believers in fulfilling the biblical pattern of unity between Jewish and Gentile believers in *Yeshua*/Jesus as the biblical "one new man" (see Ephesians 2:14–18).

> If Jewish people choose to believe in Yeshua, what better guard can be provided against assimilation and abandonment of Jewish identity than Messianic Judaism? The question of Jesus' identity should be able to

be discussed without the baggage of two millennia of Gentile Christendom that often departed starkly from Jesus' own message. I believe that Messianic Judaism provides that bridge, a witness for Yeshua to the Jewish people, and for the Jewish people to Gentile Christians. (208)

Meanwhile abroad, animosity continues to swirl around Jerusalem. Hostility against Israel's very existence smolders among her Middle Eastern neighbors. America's former warmth toward the one democracy in the Middle East seems to be at risk. One can't help wondering why those called the chosen people are perpetually resented yet today, our next subject.

11

Why are God's chosen people perpetually resented?

Representing God to the world has been a difficult assignment. God himself is deeply hated, so it is no wonder that his representatives would be hated too. Becoming the world's "scapegoat" has meant perpetual suffering for Jewish communities. Being one of the chosen people has been so grueling that many have opted out from the assignment, and some, like Karl Marx, have even fought against it. When God's Son was Incarnated, Jesus too was hated. He warned his followers that they would be hated too (see Matthew 10:22; John 15:18).

Christians Pay a Price for Being "Chosen" Also

Notice that the gift of "chosenness" was also inherited by the Gentile "branches" who were grafted into the Jewish "root" (see Romans 11:17, 18). In writing to mixed Jewish and Gentile churches, Peter addressed them all as "chosen according to the foreknowledge of God . . . for obedience to Jesus Christ."

> As you come to him, the living Stone—rejected by men
> but chosen by God and precious to him—you also, like
> living stones, are being built into a spiritual house to be
> a holy priesthood, offering spiritual sacrifices accept-
> able to God through Jesus Christ. (1 Peter 2:4–5)

Over the centuries, believers who stayed true to the Word of God were often decried, persecuted, and exiled. Martyrs were burned at the stake even by Gentile Christendom's leaders. In the last century, more martyrs have died for their faith in Jesus than in all centuries put together. Comfortable Americans barely realize the horrific price millions of Christians in other countries are paying to stay true to their commitment to the Savior.

Whole nations have rebelled against the Creator, the God of Abraham, and have chosen idols and substitute gods. Jews and Christians today share in similar suffering because they are thought to represent the God against whom the world has generally rebelled.

What "God" is the True God?

God is whoever created the world. There can only be one true, single God. How does the Creator reveal himself to humanity? By his creation of nature, and by his written message. In the Torah, God kept identifying and explaining himself by name after name. He made a covenant with one pilot people who he sovereignly chose, and repeatedly identified himself with them as "the God of Abraham, Isaac, and Jacob." His divine covenant was made with one chosen people, in one chosen land, with one chosen center, Jerusalem (see Genesis 15:12–21, 17:1–8; Deuteronomy 7:6–9; 2 Chronicles 6:5–6). At his chosen time, God revealed himself in human form. *Yeshua* commanded his chosen people to start in Jerusalem and take the message of salvation out to the whole world. What has been their response? Gentiles have largely resented the prerogative of a sovereign God, not realizing it was to meet their crucial need that one single vehicle of revelation and salvation had to be chosen.

"Chosenness"—Why Necessary?

Desiring to be in fellowship with humanity on earth, God devised a way to come to us that would not overcome us. Our Creator would eventually visit us in the Incarnation of the Messiah, but the divine Deliverer had also to be human, a second Adam (see Romans 5:12–20; 1 Corinthians 15:21–22). A family had to be chosen for this assignment, and Abraham's story shows us that choice's beginning. Abraham's family, like the whole world, had inherited the sin nature that began at the Fall. Pride and jealousy became endemic to humanity then, as it still is now. So, the Torah tells the story of jealousies within the Abrahamic family and from their surrounding cousins and pagan nations.

Perpetual Resentment of God's Chosen Sons

In the Messianic family's history, we read story after story of jealousy of the *chosen son* even within the family. Examples? Isaac and Ishmael, Jacob and Esau, Joseph and his brothers, Moses and his brother and sister, Saul, David, and finally the Messianic Son Jesus.

If we turn our lens to those who interacted with the Messianic family, we see that jealousy and hatred bled out further, with story after story of encounters between Israel and her neighbors. Examples? Egyptians, Ammonites, Moabites, Edomites, Philistines, Assyrians, Babylonians, Rome, Nazis, and more.

If we look at ongoing history, a long and consistent trail of resentment, rejection, persecution, and extermination has continued throughout the ages. Examples? Banishment from Rome, Spain, Morocco. Ghetto containments, pogroms in Russia, Holocaust in Germany. This resentment escalated to horrific proportions in Hitler's Aryan race obsession.

There was definitely something satanic behind it: a passionate rebellion against God himself for having given us a conscience and for making us accountable to him as Judge. Only the mind of a person possessed by hatred could say, as Hitler said to Rauschning, "Conscience is a Jewish invention!" and "There is no room for two chosen peoples!" (Basilea Schlink, *Israel My Chosen People: A German Confession before God and the Jews*, 13).

If we picture today's situation, we find the small state of Israel surrounded by Muslim neighbors who openly state their intention to wipe her from the face of the earth. The United Nations vote to call her day of becoming a nation "the Day of Catastrophe" is a summary statement of Israel's rejection today.

God's Assignment to the Chosen

The Scriptures tell us that God chose one family to emulate a society whose way of life was to be holy and compassionate. Examples? His Ten Commandments for harmonious communal living (see Exodus 20:1–17). Knowing fallen humanity's propensity to sin, God arranged for a societal renewal every fifty years. The Jubilee's reorganization of the nation was to overcome misuses that had accrued over time by freeing any who had become debtors and slaves and bringing everyone back to possess their original homesteads. Isaiah revealed God's role for Israel related to Gentiles in God's own words:

> I the Lord have called you in righteousness; I will take hold of your hand. I will keep you and will make you to be a covenant for the people, a light for the Gentiles, to open eyes that are blind, to free captives from prison, and to release from the dungeon those who sit in darkness. (Isaiah 42:6–7)

However, the Messianic family failed to stay true to their calling. The Old Testament records sagas of Israel's unfaithfulness as they worshiped the idols of their surrounding neighbors. Then came God's discipline, followed by their restoration and revival, but repeatedly their spiritual decline (see Daniel 9; Nehemiah 9).

The Incarnation: Rejection of the *Living* Word of God

The God of Abraham, Isaac, and Jacob sent the Son to earth. But even though his life and miracles clearly demonstrated his identity, his own people's leadership rejected him and turned him over to the Romans to be crucified. "He came to his own, but his own received him not" (John 1:11a). A few thousand Jews did receive him, and soon even more Gentiles were accepted in Hebrew churches. Early believers in *Yeshua* were a minority in Israel, and even today only a minority of the Messianic family in the world embrace him as the LORD's Christ (i.e., Messiah).

Behind Hatred of God's Eternal Love for His Chosen

Satan's war against God that started in Genesis looks generally successful today. Idols of all types are widely worshiped. The Enemy would not want us to be aware of what God has revealed in his Word about the final chapter of the world's story of rebellion. Throughout Scripture, the Day of the LORD has been predicted. The certainty of the end of time as we know it has been made clear in both Testaments. We wonder whether humanity's day of reckoning may be close, which is our next subject.

12

What is on the horizon for all nations?

It would be strange for thinking people today not to be concerned about our own and the world's future. We seem to be floundering in uncharted waters, wondering about the future of our planet, considering the break-down of nations, borders, civility, health, climate, economics, culture, politics, morality, and more. They all seem to be converging with such speed that we feel out of control. If all that were not enough, add the threats of digitized money, "social credit" control, the World Economic Forum's plans for world-wide government, plus the unknown threats of Artificial Intelligence.

Cascading Specters

As Jonathan Cahn has perceived in his book, *The Return of the Gods*, even in formerly "Christianized" Europe and America, we are experiencing the return of the pagan gods. The world is drowning in false religions and lostness. Jesus predicted that when judgment would finally fall, the godless world would resemble the times of Noah, the time when "The Lord saw how great man's wickedness on the earth had become, and that every inclination of the thoughts of his heart was only evil all the time" (Genesis 6:5).

Daily our TVs show us murders, riots, wars, atrocities, refugee camps, prisons, churches burned, cities bombed, children starving, and more. Nationhood is tottering and global government is being proposed. The Deceiver would not want us to remember that no autocratic ruler yet has proved incorruptible. The scenario seems to be lining up for what the Bible calls the rule of the antichrist.

Especially through the media, today's prevailing Western culture is rejecting and mocking God's plan for human flourishing. Sexuality is becoming obsessive and perverted. The Bible is accused and rejected. God's principles are flouted, right down to the human family. Revolt against the gender we are born with pushes human rebellion back to Creation. Healthy affections are being smashed. Humans are encouraged to mate indiscriminately like animals. Holy living is mocked. Both genders are becoming at risk from each other. Resistance to manipulation is waning. Elite consortiums are openly preparing to rule the world, i.e., to replace God. Technologies are being developed which threaten to be turned loose as conscienceless tools. Even nature is groaning. It is no wonder that fear and depression are rampant.

Sudden Destruction

As of October 7, 2023, Israel has suffered another holy day surprise attack, exactly fifty years after their neighboring countries' assault on Israel's Yom Kipper holy day in 1973. Its barbaric nature bears the marks of demonic origin. Its perpetrators' intended wider conflagration further threatens our reeling world.

Only God Knows and Is Able to Predict the Future

Is there no good news? Providentially God says there is. We wonder, what does the future hold? Since humans can imagine, but are unable to really know the future, we turn to the only all-knowing One: God. His revealed history, the Bible, is our resource for learning what has happened in the past, and his prophetic word is our only source for what will happen in the future.

Fulfillment is a theme that runs throughout Scripture—completion of God's goal. Jesus said he came to *"fulfill* the law" (see Matthew 5:17). Matthew's Gospel speaks repeatedly of what was predicted by the prophets being *fulfilled* in the Messiah (Examples: Matthew 2:15, 23, 3:15, 4:14, etc.).

Biblical Feasts Reveal Progression Toward Fulfillment

One category of predicted fulfillments is based on God's sacred calendar. The "feasts unto the LORD" are ordained in Exodus 12:11–28, 23:14–17; Leviticus 16, 23, 25; Numbers 28, 29; Deuteronomy 16, and appear throughout the Bible. A forty-page section of my study titled *The Messiah Mystery: The Old and New Testaments' Inseparable Disclosure* examines the feasts' fulfillments by the Lord Jesus.

When God delivered his community out of captivity to Pharaoh's schedule and rule, he completely reorganized and recalibrated the Hebrews' lives. Having created Time, God set up a lunar calendar for their years. Feasts were carefully timed in relationship to the agricultural seasons, and usually were enjoyed at full moon. Three of the seven were consecutive in the spring, one in early summer, and three together in the fall. They progressed toward the year's goal, the Ingathering. Seven times seven years made forty-nine and proceeded toward the Jubilee's goal of restoring all societal damages in order to start with a clean slate at the fiftieth year. (The book *Jubilee Journey: Hope for Now to Eternity* was my way of examining this pattern and applying it to our own lives today.)

The appointed "feasts unto the LORD" were teaching times to draw God's people to himself. *Yeshua* used these gatherings at the Temple in Jerusalem as platforms for revealing his identity. John 7 is an example. Most striking is the week of the Lamb of God's crucifixion and resurrection. They took place on the exact timetable of the first three feasts. At the exact week of the Passover, Jesus gave his blood as the Passover lamb (*Pesach*). His sinless body was broken and buried on the exact day of Unleavened Bread. He came forth from the grave on the exact day of First Fruits on that year's calendar.

Exactly fifty days later at the Feast of Weeks, God poured out the Holy Spirit upon all believers (*Shavuot*). Significantly, those first four feasts were completed on the exact dates that matched God's calendar. Impossible timing unless God ordained! On the basis of these careful fulfillments, it is reasonable to expect the last three to match his calendar as well. (*Rosh Hashanah, Yom Kipper, Sukkot*—i.e., Trumpets, Day of Atonement, Tabernacles.)

The feasts are like the drama of the ages played out in three acts with seven scenes. Unfinished aspects appear in "shadowy form" until they happen. It is natural to wonder where we are on God's timeline. We can be sure that God will keep his promises. His Messiah is the marker. We can be confident that eventually "the times will have reached their fulfillment."

> And he made known to us the mystery of his will according to his good pleasure, which he purposed in Christ, to be put into effect when the times will have reached their fulfillment—to bring all things in heaven and on earth together under one head, even Christ. (Ephesians 1:9–10)

Prophecy: God's Tool to Test Authenticity and Give Warning

People have always wished for light on the future. Prophetic passages play a part in nearly a fourth of the Bible, and yet they are often ignored. God's exact fulfillment of prophesied events are repeatedly recorded in the Old Testament by historically verifiable times, places, rulers, and events.

The exact fulfillment of a prophecy was God's supreme method of authentication. It proved who was a true prophet speaking by the Spirit of God, and who was presumptively making up predictions falsely. The authentic Old Testament prophets were generally rejected by their hearers.

Not only in Old Testament times, but even now humanity tends to disregard what God has revealed. If we do choose to believe him, God's Word gives us many clues about the world's future. The Lord Jesus provided a whole body of revelation about what to expect near the end of the age in Matthew 24 and 25, Mark 13, Luke 21, and finally in the book of Revelation. When God "calls time," judgment will finally take place. Jesus repeatedly advised his own, "Be always on the watch and pray that you will be able to escape all that is about to happen, and that you may be able to stand before the Son of Man" (Luke 21:35).

The Return of Christ

The timing of the Lord's return is debated among Christians. Jesus promised it in John 14:1–3. What is called "the Rapture" is based on a passage in Paul's letter to the Thessalonian church:

> For the Lord himself will come down from heaven, with a loud command, with the voice of the archangel and with the trumpet call of God, and the dead in Christ will rise first. After that, we who are still alive and are left will be caught up together with them in the clouds to meet the Lord in the air. And so we will be with the Lord forever. Therefore encourage each other with these words. (1 Thessalonians 4:16)

Prophecies Related to Gentiles and Jews

An eventual transition is predicted to come, one that will affect Jews and Gentiles. The ultimate Prophet, Jesus, revealed that "Jerusalem will be trampled on by the Gentiles until the times of the Gentiles are fulfilled" (Luke 21:24). In a related passage, the Apostle Paul grieved over his people's unbelief, and he spoke to the Gentile believers in Rome, saying:

> I do not want you to be ignorant of the mystery, brothers, so that you may not be conceited: Israel has experienced a hardening in part until the full number of Gentiles has come in. And so all Israel will be saved, . . . As far as the gospel is concerned, they are enemies on your account; but as far as election is concerned, they are loved on account of the patriarchs, for God's gifts and his call are irrevocable. (Romans 11:25–26a, 28–29)

What can supersessionists make of this prediction? If the Hebrew people were totally replaced, why does Scripture predict a future for Israel? And what about the era called the "Millennium"—the summary term for the "one thousand years" mentioned five times in Revelation 20? These years are spoken of as a period when Satan will be bound (see Revelation 20:2) and Christ will reign along with the resurrected martyrs who ". . . had been beheaded because of their testimony for Jesus and for the word of God" (Revelation 20:4b).

Various Interpretations of "the Millennium"

It is important to clarify two frequently misunderstood terms that are used to summarize two opposite views about the future event called the Millennium: "Amillennial" and "Premillennial." Although variations of these viewpoints are complicated, their general differences grow out of either belief in, or rejection of, replacement theology. Those who base their theology on replacement's dismissal of all things Jewish do not accept a literal fulfillment of a reign of the Son of David in Jerusalem. Therefore, their designation is called "amillennial"—"a" meaning "no"—so no millennium, or if there is one, the Church right now is itself the rule of Christ. Those who take Scripture more literally expect the fulfillment to be initiated by the return of the Messiah, and hence are called "premillennial"—"pre" meaning "before"—that the King will return first, to bring his reign to fruition.

Many church goers are not even familiar with these two terms, yet they inherit their presuppositions. Admirably, many of this generation's churched young people seem to deeply desire to change the world for the better. Those with an amillennial background tend to give themselves to the challenge of repairing all elements of the social order. Those with a premillennial viewpoint tend to focus more on evangelism, taking Christ's commission to heart:

> All authority in heaven and earth has been given to me. Therefore go and make disciples of all nations, baptizing them in the name of the Father and of the Son and of the Holy Spirit, and teaching them to obey everything I have commanded you. And surely I am with you always to the very end of the age. (Matthew 28:18b–20)

"Nations" (i.e., Gentiles) keep being distinguished from Israel in the Bible. Jesus predicted, "When the Son of Man comes in all his glory, . . . All nations will be gathered before him, and he will separate the people one from another as a shepherd separates the sheep from the goats" (Matthew 25:31a, 32).

Luke's account of what Jesus revealed about the signs of the end includes a startling fact: "Jerusalem will be trampled on by the Gentiles until the times of the Gentiles are fulfilled" (Luke 21:24). That causes us to wonder how close we are to the end of the times of the Gentiles.

The Jew/Gentile distinction is noticeable in the book of Revelation. The first three chapters are warnings to the Apostle John's seven contemporary churches located in what is present-day Turkey—largely Gentile congregations. Those glimpsed worshiping at God's throne in Heaven are from every tribe and nation (see Revelation 5:9, 7:9). After that, throughout most of Revelation's middle chapters, the Church is never mentioned. The prophetic future reveals a markedly Jewish-focused period during the Tribulation.

Are all these Jewish-related terms to be taken literally or not? Some who take the metaphorical view of Revelation taught by replacement theology would see the "twelve tribes of Israel and the one-hundred and forty-four thousand" in Revelation 7:4–8 and 14:1 to really mean the Church.

Those who expect the Scriptures' predictions to be literally fulfilled look forward to Israel finally recognizing her long-lost brother. They yearn for the time predicted in Zechariah:

> And I will pour out on the house of David and the inhabitants of Jerusalem a spirit of grace and supplication. They will look on me, the one they have pierced, and they will mourn for him as one mourns for an only child, and grieve bitterly for him as one mourns for a firstborn son. (Zechariah 12:10)

Expecting prophecy to be actually fulfilled helps believers take comfort that the generation will finally come when the revelation given Paul that "all Israel will be saved" will finally happen and be proven true (see Romans 11:26).

Glimpses of the Climax of History

After the old world comes to its close, God promises joyful restoration to those who have received the Savior he sent: a new heaven and a new earth where God will dwell with his people.

> He will wipe every tear from their eyes. There will be no more death or mourning or crying or pain. For the old order of things has passed away. He who was seated on the throne said, "I am making everything new." Then he said, "Write this down, for these words are trustworthy and true." (Revelation 21:4–5)

At last, the prayer that *Yeshua* taught—"your kingdom come, your will be done" (Matthew 6:10)—will be answered. By God's merciful grace, his goal for Jew and Gentile will have been achieved.

The Lord Jesus revealed what to expect before his return. "Just as it was in the days of Noah, so it will be in the days of the Son of man. People were eating and drinking, buying and selling, marrying and being given in marriage up to the day Noah entered the ark. Then the flood came and destroyed them all" (Luke 17:26–27). In his overview of what would happen between his first coming as Savior and second coming as King, Jesus gave us these sobering facts:

> Nation will rise against nation, and kingdom against kingdom. There will be famines and earthquakes in various places. All these are the beginnings of birth pains. Then you will be handed over to be persecuted and put to death because of me. At that time many will turn away from the faith and will betray and hate each other, and many false prophets will appear and deceive many people. Because of the increase of wickedness, the love of most will grow cold, but he who stands to the end will be saved. And the gospel of the kingdom will be preached in the whole world as a testimony to all nations, and then the end will come. (Matthew 24:7–14)

In Jesus' book of Revelation, we glimpse the dreadful Tribulation and then a glorious renewal of all things. How much is plain description and how much is metaphor, only God knows. But even that which is metaphor represents God's truth, not figments of human imagination (see 2 Peter 1:20).

The Messianic King's Wedding

Jesus had told parables hinting at his eventual wedding to those who choose to love Him (see Luke 14:16–24; Matthew 22:2–14, 25:1–13). The wedding of the Lamb is foreseen in Revelation 19.

The Bridegroom coming "soon" for his Bride identifies himself as the "Root and Offspring of David" (see Revelation 22:16). Their home is called "the new Jerusalem." Its gates are named for the twelve tribes of Israel, and the names of the twelve Apostles of the Lamb are written on the city's foundations (see Revelation 21:14). The Apostle John points out that "I did not see a temple in the city, because the Lord God Almighty and the Lamb are its temple" (Revelation 21:22). Gentile believers can also rejoice because of the promise that "The glory and honor of the nations will be brought into it" (Revelation 21:26).

Things so amazing as God's creation of the world and Jesus' resurrection from the dead are either true or false. Correspondingly, things so amazing as the creation of a new world and our potential presence within it are also either true or false.

Reality Check

Taking the Lord Jesus' predictions seriously, what can we deduce from what we know of the world's situation today? How close do our times seem to resemble the "times of Noah" that he predicted would be the situation at the coming of the Son of Man? (see Matthew 24:37). Where do we seem to be on the spectrum of history? God's Ten Commandments for human good are being forgotten, and even his sovereign creation of humanity as "male and female" in his image is being denied. Persecution and martyrdom of Christians over the world in this current century number more than in all time before. Wars and earthquakes increasingly shake our world. Second Timothy's prophecy paints a familiar picture of attitudes today:

> But mark this: There will be terrible times in the last days. People will be lovers of themselves, lovers of money, boastful, proud, abusive, disobedient to their parents, ungrateful, unholy, without love, unforgiving, slanderous, without self-control, brutal, not lovers of the good, treacherous, rash, conceited, lovers of

pleasure rather than lovers of God, having a form of godliness but denying its power." (2 Timothy 3:1–5a)

Positive Signs of Nearing Completion

Thankfully, there are also encouraging signs that were predicted to precede the return of the Lord Jesus Christ. First, but little recognized, is the significance that in our own generation, after two thousand years, Israel is back in the land. Jews scattered over the world's continents for centuries are "making aliya" back to their Homeland. One of the most dramatic returns is that of the Ethiopian Falasha community. "The Black Jew Enigma" is a chapter in *Overcomers*, my 2018 book chronicling God's deliverances of Christians and Jews during Ethiopia's Marxist Revolution.

Second, as reported in preceding chapters, the Messianic Jewish movement is growing. Many Jews are already singing, "Blessed is he who comes in the name of the Lord." The Messiah, weeping over his rejection, spoke of his return:

> O Jerusalem, Jerusalem, you who kill the prophets and stone those sent to you, how often I have longed to gather your children together, as a hen gathers her chicks under her wings, but you were not willing. Look, your house is left to you desolate. For I tell you, you will not see me again until you say, "Blessed is he who comes in the name of the Lord." (Matthew 23:37–39)

Third, among Gentile believers, getting the Gospel to "the ends of the earth" as Jesus commissioned his community to do in Acts 1:9 is burgeoning forward through technological advances and new third-world emissaries spreading out over the globe. Amazingly, due to the speed of technology, distributors of the *Jesus Film* (the book of Luke) tell us that translations of the film are by now making the Gospel available in the languages of 97 percent of the world's people.

Why So Long Delayed?

Just like the disciples in the first century AD, we also ask, "When will the Lord return?" In Acts 1:7, *Yeshua* disclosed that even he did not know, and that only the Father knew. His reply was consistent with the marriage customs of Galilee. The engaged son was to go home and build a room on the father's home, and the father would decide when the son could go to get his bride.

One wonders if Christ's delayed coming is related to the Church's distraction and lack of fulfillment of his commission to reach all nations, after which he said, "the end will come" (see Matthew 24:14). Actually, the "end" refers to the fallen world's end, after which comes the promise of the "beginning" of a restored new world! (see Revelation 21)

The Deeper Question

Throughout our consideration of previous questions, repeatedly we've been asking "why?" By now we may realize that perhaps the ultimate question we should be asking is not "why," but something else.

13

Why is "why" not our most crucial question?

The preceding chapters have focused mainly on *"why"* questions. Are there other questions that could help us decipher their deeper indications? Would it be prudent to face their personal implications for our own lives?

What If?

One way to re-evaluate these issues' histories is to re-image their antithesis. Using another lens, we could ask not *"why"* but *"what if?"*

- What if the early Jewish believers in Jesus had not been displaced by the Gentile-ization of the faith?

- What if Constantine had not diluted and neutralized the *ecclesia* by wedding church and state?

- What if the sword had not been used to convert and kill?

- What if Augustine's metaphorical interpretation had not led to amillennial interpretations of Scripture that caused Gentile Christian "branches" to dismiss the Bible's Jewishness?

- What if the Gospel of God's grace had simply continued to spread from person to person as described in Acts

2:42–47, with people being added to the church day by day? Might the Jewish and Gentile unity of the *ecclesia* have been maintained, drawing others into their accepting and loving community?

- What if the original burgeoning Jesus movement had continued its contagious way throughout the world, speeding Jesus' prediction that the Gospel would be preached to all nations, and then the end would come? (see Matthew 24:14) Might our Lord's return have come sooner?

- What if the Inquisition, Crusades, pogroms, deportations, ghettos, and other de-humanizations that led to the Holocaust had never happened? Might Jewish and Gentile believers in Jesus have remained united, expressing the continuity and unity of both Covenants?

But no, these "what ifs" did not happen. God gives humanity the freedom of choice. We are inheriting our ancestors' sins and mistakes, and we commit our own. Rather than *why* or *what if,* could *who* be our most essential question to raise?

Who Gave Man the Freedom of Choice?

Our confusion pushes us back to human history's beginning. God revealed the origin of our problem in the book of Genesis. The first chapters of the Bible explain life's most basic problem. We need to ask "who." In Genesis 3, God's enemy took aim to destroy the relationship between the world's Creator and those he had created "in his image." Man's nature was damaged in what we call "the Fall." Thereafter, an unseen and largely unrecognized spiritual war has continued throughout human history, always destroying unity between God and man, tribe and tribe, male and female, parents and children. Various surrogates of Satan, "antichrists," strut across history, envying, dividing, spoiling, twisting, angering, lying, hating, perverting, and murdering humanity (see 1 John 2:18–23, 4:1–3).

The Hebrews as a Case Study

In the Old Testament, God gave his guidelines for harmonious living and recorded a case study of the one chosen Messianic family within humanity, that of Abraham. When we delve into Israel's history, we find that most of the kings of both Divided Kingdoms strayed from worshiping the God of Abraham and turned to Amorite gods—Baal, Asherah poles, and calf worship. Leaders like Jeroboam are repeatedly cited as having "caused Israel to sin" (see 1 Kings 16:19).

Worldwide Case Study

Israel's unfaithfulness is a case study that is repeated in the wider world. It is rare to find a Gentile leader who has not been corrupted by power. Consider our world's leadership today. Look at America's political turmoil. Messianic Jew Jonathan Cahn, in his recent book, *The Return of the Gods*, (applying Jesus' parable in Luke 11:24–26), shows America's Gentile mirror reflection of Israel's record. At first, America swept out false gods and dedicated its house to the worship of God, but then swept Him out and left the house empty. Therefore, seven worse demons have rushed in. They resemble the same gods that defiled Israel: "calf worship" of nature, "Baal's" sacrifice of children, "Molech's" passion for war, and "Asherah's" perversion of sex.

The convergence of disasters on so many world-wide fronts today possibly portend the apocalyptic climax predicted in the book of God's Revelation. Biblical prerequisites are falling into place. Israel is back in the land. Jerusalem is the political world's focal point again. The means for the whole world to "see" events at one time is digitally possible. Demonic hatreds and perversions are spiraling throughout the world. Artificial Intelligence threatens humanity with a loss of truth, reality, privacy, protection, freedom, usefulness, and more.

Jews are again under attack. The American nation that once attempted to lay her foundations in line with the Word of God is now promoting godlessness. This makes our culture doubly guilty, having had access to God's true truth and now throwing it away.

Who Instigates Rebellion Against God?

Who is behind all this carnage? Who is it who hates the Creator? Who wants to divide and destroy us? Who is behind today's envies, wars, retaliations, power politics, and moral collapse? Who would want to kill the unborn, sexualize little children, entice into addictions, ruin marriages, destroy the family, decimate humanity? Who incites people to either blame God for what we have done, or hide by declaring him non-existent? The obvious answer leads us to Satan. We ask "Who can defeat humanity's foe?" Only God! "But how can we connect with the Almighty's deliverance?"

Who Can Deliver Us?

First of all, let's consider: Who is God? Creation displays the Creator's power and beauty, but what reveals his mind and heart? To employ a human example, separated people share their minds and hearts with their loved ones through the miracle of writing. Likewise, through the Scriptures, God reveals his heart. He has recorded his pilgrimage with the world that he loves so dearly that he sent his Son to redeem all those who the Tempter has charmed, used, and seeks to destroy. With all our education and technology, we humans prove ourselves still unable to create beneficent governments who can actually protect us from our selfish sins against each other, and their attending miseries. Yet in the face of our multiple Jewish and Gentile failures, God has mercy on us all (see Romans 11:32).

Who Is the World's Savior?

Second: What is the true identity of Jesus? A wonderful answer to this question comes from Jonathan Cahn, twice the speaker at Presidential Prayer breakfasts in Washington DC. A meditation in his *Book of Mysteries* is focused on Joseph's experience of being hated by his brothers, left in a pit, thrown into an Egyptian prison, but eventually miraculously raised to be second only to Pharoah. During a famine, Joseph's brothers come to Egypt desperate for grain. Of course, they cannot recognize Joseph, who is dressed as and speaks as an Egyptian. They can only see a lord of Egypt, a Gentile savior of a Gentile land. Consider this marvelous dialogue titled "The Mask of the Egyptian" in Jonathan Cahn's book:

> "For the last two thousand years Messiah has become the Savior to people of every nation and tongue . . . and yet, He's been estranged from His own family, Israel, the Jewish people. To them He's the Savior of the Gentiles. They can't see past the foreign clothing, the adornments . . . "

> "The stained glass, the statues, the icons, the cathedrals of a culture cut off from its Jewish roots. But that's not the end of the story. What happens at the end?"

> "Joseph's brothers finally realize that the Egyptian is their long-lost brother . . . and their hope as well."

> "So too the story of Messiah and His people will end when they stand before Him face-to-face and finally see through the clothing, the adornments, and the mask of two thousand years. And then they will realize that the Savior of the Gentiles is their long-lost brother, Yeshua, their Joseph, and their hope as well. Pray for that day. For when it comes, it will be Messiah's joy, Israel's redemption, and, as it is written, riches for the world."

> Genesis 44:18; 45:1–2; Hosea 3:4–5; Zechariah 12:10–13:1; Matthew 23:37–39 (347)

How wonderful to anticipate Jewish eyes finally opened to their brother's true identity!

What Is Humanity's Identity?

Third: Who are we? We are those to whom life on earth was gifted by the lover of our souls. But love cannot be demanded. For love to be genuine, it must be a chosen response. People— male and female created in God's image (see Genesis 1:27)— are given the power to resist or receive God's love, a love that was most deeply revealed through the full redemption from our sins that our Father provided through his anointed One, the Messiah. The Messiah's purpose was to bring salvation not only to Israel, but to the whole world. The Son of God did not come to set up a temporary kingdom in a small Middle Eastern nation. He was bringing in a Kingdom for all people, one that spans time and space, and from earth to heaven.

Who Is Actually Our Foe?

Fourth: Who is "the enemy"? It is crucial to understand that our tendency to equate "the enemy" with "those with whom we dis-agree" is a false understanding of reality. The story of mankind is a story of an ongoing war between the God who loves us and the Deceiver who hates us.

The despoiling of God's good creation started at the Fall. Biblically, Satan is called "the prince of this world" (see John 12:31, 14:30, 16:11). The Devil and his surrogates have troubled humanity from the beginning. Jesus defeated Satan on the Cross, but his ultimate end has been delayed.

Now we seem to be nearing the climax of history. Humans and even nature are agonizing. The convergence of catastrophes keeps escalating. Changes are speeding up. Truth is being de-stroyed. Now, Artificial Intelligence is on the horizon, threaten-ing to obscure the very ground of our stability. The Bible being banned by today's culture seemed a likely development, but even more diabolical would be the latest threat proposed: AI's "rewriting" the Bible. The Bible is the most comprehensive and true history of humanity. We find ourselves in a *Strange New*

World, the title of Carl R. Trueman's 2022 synopsis of how we got to this catastrophic juncture.

Life's Most Crucial Decision

Finally, we ask ourselves the most essential questions: "Who am I? Jew or Gentile though I be. Who made me? Who knows the truth? Who do I trust? Who genuinely loves me—enough to die for me? Who decides the terms of my final judgment, my final destiny?"

God's Word tells us that his desire is that no one would perish (see John 3:16; 2 Peter 3:9). He has waited patiently throughout history, giving us time to make our own choices. How sobering that Jesus predicted it would be the minority who would choose the narrow road to Life (see Matthew 7:13–14). His parables pointed to the serious choice of one's destiny. Consider the refusers of the King's invitation to the Son's wedding, warned in Matthew 22, or the ten virgins, of whom only five entered the wedding, revealed in Matthew 25.

The Destiny Each of Us Chooses

That entrance depends on whether we choose to be "married" to the King of kings, the King of the Jews, on whose head the crown of thorns was jammed by unbelief. Who will I be? Will I join those who decry him as an imposter, or bond with those who love him as their Savior?

Oh, how sad to miss the Bridegroom King's love during life on earth. How woeful in the end to fail to share in his Bride's eternal inheritance! So, we ask ourselves, "From the two contenders for human souls, to whose kingdom do I make my choice to belong . . . today . . . and therefore throughout eternity?"

God has given us a window into the future in the last two chapters of the book of Revelation. Oh, dear believing Jew, oh, ingrafted Gentile, we will be fully reconciled when we meet at the Marriage Feast of the Lamb. How wonderful to anticipate the consummation that God's Word promises—joys beyond description. How amazing to enter into his New Jerusalem, all renewed, healed, and beautiful, no longer marred by pain or death. How marvelous to anticipate blessed reunions with those loved in the past and begin new adventures in Eternity's future!

14

Oh, Jewish and Gentile believers, one in the Lord, a plea!

Understanding our painful and convoluted history helps us to better realize what the Enemy of God has done to estrange our communities from each other. The Devil's "wolves in sheep's clothing" have scattered the flock, leaving most Jews and Gentiles wandering in unbelieving wilderness, cut off from the Good Shepherd, *Yeshua*.

The whole world has suffered from unholy rejection of God's truth and God's people. Unbelieving Jewish leadership initially rejected the Lord's Christ, and Gentile leadership soon rejected the Lord's Chosen People. We inherit this legacy. The Enemy who "makes war against the woman's offspring and believers in Jesus" would seek to keep us divided (see Revelation 12:17).

Unity Provided, but Resisted

But the One stronger than Satan has already provided for our union. To Gentiles was given the promise that "... now in Christ Jesus you who once were far away have been brought near by the blood of Christ. For he himself is our peace, who has made the two one and has destroyed the barrier, ... His purpose was to create in himself one new man out of the two, thus making peace through the cross, by which he put to death their hostility" (see Ephesians 2:13, 14a, 15b, 16).

We forget or resist God's provision for our unity. Even those who trust in Jesus still struggle with lingering animosities and resentments that cripple our witness to the world. Both communities' leadership rejected the true Messiah, Israel's during the Incarnation, Christendom's during her apostate wanderings. Jealous Gentiles have envied the "chosen" brother and sought to replace Israel. Believing Jews still resist union with the *ecclesia's* largely Gentile believers.

Nearing the End of the Gentile Age?

And yet God seems to be doing a new thing in our own generation. We may be arriving at the scripturally predicted "end of the Gentile age" (see Luke 21:24; Romans 11:25). The signs of the times and Israel's restoration to the land point to the Lord's return. "Just as man is destined to die once, so Christ was sacrificed once to take away the sins of many people; and he will appear a second time, not to bear sin, but to bring salvation to those who are waiting for him" (Hebrews 9:27–28). When the Incarnated Jesus wept over Jerusalem's unbelief, he anticipated His second coming: "For I tell you, you will not see me again until you say, 'Blessed is he who comes in the name of the Lord'" (Matthew 23:39; see Psalm 118:26).

How should our generation of believers prepare for his return? Should we not reflect the union he died to accomplish? Are Gentile believers not responsible to admit Christendom's flaws, repent for our replacement error, and ask forgiveness from the Hebrew community? Are Jewish believers not responsible to welcome the wild branches into their natural olive tree? Are there ways our communities can begin to purposefully develop relationships together?

This is a time for repentance and reconciliation by both the root and branch faith communities. Scripture teaches us that the salvation which the Savior accomplished has united us as "one new man." That marvelous unity has been damaged and even denied for centuries. Interestingly, at this prophetic moment in history two thousand years after the Jerusalem Council of Acts 15, a few believers are thinking about the need for a second Jerusalem Council to reaffirm God's truth and correct our relationship with each other.

This thought-provoking initiative goes by the acrostic TJCII—meaning "Toward Jerusalem Council II." The One New Man project can be investigated at https://rabbittrailproductions.com/onenewmanseries. The series documents the history of Jewish/Gentile relationships since the Incarnation, shows the influence of replacement theology, explores the history of TJCII, encourages repentance for wrongs done to the Jewish people, and promotes reconciliation between people of different denominations.

In a related book, Willem J. Ouweneel in *The Eternal People* reminds all of us of our mutual guilts:

> Around the year 30, hundreds of Jerusalem Jews killed "our" Lord; this is horrible. But hundreds of millions of "Christians" have killed six million Jews—is this less horrible? There can be no shared future for Jews and Christians under the one God of Israel unless each group confesses its guilt—acknowledging the "Christian" guilt is unspeakably much larger than Jewish guilt. (146)

Who can help us come together in godly repentance and reconciliation? Only the Lord's Spirit.

The Role of the New Bridge-Crossing Movement

Who has God freshly visited in redemption at this late hour in history? Jews! The recent rise of the Messianic Jewish Movement is a sign of the Spirit's moving anew in our day. Jews who recognize who *Yeshua* was and is can walk over the bridge to Gentile believers. Our shared Messiah is the bridge—not Christianity, nor Judaism, nor a movement, but Messiah himself. He is our peace with God and with each other. We who have been blessed by this reconciliation are to proclaim the good news of *Yeshua's* resurrection and his redemption offered to the unbelieving world. Our testimony would be far more believable if we evidenced Spirit-provided love for each other.

Although these chapters have been critical of Christendom, we need to affirm the Bridegroom's love for his true Bride, the true *ecclesia* for whom Christ died—both Jewish and Gentile believers bonded together by genuinely loving the Lover of our souls.

In Conclusion

Dear Reader, I hope these Jewish and Gentile "why" questions have helped each of us to face where Christendom got the big story of the Scriptures wrong. These facts are hard to recognize and admit. Some surely will disagree. The biblical references given, and the books listed in the bibliography, offer sources for those moved to investigate further.

Nevertheless, seeing the collateral damage through these lenses may help us to better understand where each viewpoint is coming from, and may clarify why. No matter from which background you have come, may these possible explanations offer viewpoints that are worth considering. They challenge our faithfulness to the whole Word of God. The issues raised affect the entire Jewish and Gentile people of God, and their implications spill out all over the world.

None of us has full understanding. Each can contribute to the whole. God's truth is so deep, and our grasp is so shallow, that what any of us concludes is partial at best. "Now we see but a poor reflection as in a mirror; then we shall see face to face.

Now we know in part; then I shall know fully, even as I am fully known" (1 Corinthians 13:12).

The Apostle Paul found it necessary to admonish quarreling believers in Corinth, saying,

> "What I mean is this: One of you says, 'I follow Paul'; another, 'I follow Apollos'; another, 'I follow Cephas'; still another, 'I follow Christ.' Is Christ divided? Was Paul crucified for you?" (1 Corinthians 1:12, 13b)

The Savior's people were to be known by their deep love for each other. Shamefully, we've generally been known by our recriminations and separations. Furthermore, we have undiscerningly let divisions fester and destroy.

Jewish brothers have mistreated their own Messiah, and Gentile Christians have mistreated their Messiah's family. Over and over in the accounts given to us in both Testaments, God calls us to recognize and admit where we have gone wrong. Then he can blot out our sins through the atonement he has provided and become our Restorer.

What are the sins we have tried to be honest about facing together? The Old Testament records a long series of the Abrahamic Covenant community's "wilderness wanderings" both in the desert and in the land. The New Testament warns Jesus' believers not to lapse into the unfaithfulness that the New Covenant community could expect to face if they too wandered in an apostate wilderness. God's patience with the Jewish saga from Abraham to the Messiah covered two thousand years. His patience with the Gentile age now comes to another two thousand years.

We have considered that biblically speaking, we may be coming to the close of the age of the Gentiles. Jesus predicted that "the gospel of the Kingdom will be preached in the whole world as a testimony to all nations, and then the end will come" (Matthew 24:14).

We are saddened by the failures of both communities of faith. When the Jewish Apostle Paul wrote to Gentile believers in Rome, he pondered the mystery of Jewish spiritual blindness and its relationship to Gentiles. We have tried to honestly face what the Spirit revealed to both communities in Romans 11. Let us marvel with Paul at the Spirit's summary in verse 12: "God has bound all men over to disobedience so that he may have mercy on them all." What patience, what love, what forgiveness, and what mercy!

As we review the Old Testament's un-laundered record of Jewish history, and try to piece together the Church's blemished history, there are faithful and heroic exceptions, but much needs to be admitted as regretful. God's mercy has been poured out on us all. Bottom line, we have all been under attack by an unseen Enemy. His attempts at destruction began in Genesis and his goal is glimpsed in Revelation 12:17: "Then the dragon was enraged and went off to make war against the rest of her offspring—those who obey God's commands and hold to the testimony of Jesus."

As we experience our estrangement, our attempts at understanding, admission, and confession are desperately needed. But such is the human heart that we are helpless to bring forth reconciliation by our own determination. We must humbly call on the Spirit of God to transform us.

In order to see the forest but not be blinded by the trees, Carl R. Truman's 2022 book, *Strange New World,* helps us face the enemy's devices at work in our situation today. Truman's book is sort of a primer on the history of how the world went mad. But after explaining the roots of the diabolical dysfunctions that face us, the author concludes:

> This is not a time for hopeless despair nor naïve optimism. Yes, let's lament the ravages of the fall as they play out in distinctive ways that our generation has chosen, but let that lamentation be the context for

shaping our identity as the people of God and our hunger for the great consummation that awaits at the feast of the Lamb. (186–187)

Oh, beloved Jew, oh adopted Gentile, let us repent for our rebellion against the God who loves us so. Let us forgive and love one another *now*. We soon may be increasingly marginalized and criminalized as we signify the Judeo/Christian God to other faiths and re-paganized cultures. From the book of Revelation we can expect that Jewish and Gentile believers in the Creator and in Jesus will increasingly not be tolerated. Yet the lives of those who represent him can shine all the more brightly in today's darkness. It is time to draw together in humility, reconciliation, and love. Whether chosen or adopted, together we will be strengthened by the Word of God and empowered by his Spirit who indwells all his people.

It was from prison in the first century that the Apostle to the Gentiles sent this message to the ethnically mixed believers in Ephesus:

> Therefore, remember that formerly you who are Gentiles by birth and called "uncircumcised" by "the circumcision" (that done in the body by the hands of men)—remember that at that time you were separate from Christ, excluded from citizenship in Israel and foreigners to the covenants of the promise, without hope and without God in the world. But now in Christ Jesus you who once were far away have now been brought near through the blood of Christ.
>
> For he himself is our peace, who has made the two of us one and has destroyed the barrier, the dividing wall of hostility, by abolishing in his flesh the law with its commandments and regulations. His purpose was to create in himself one new man out of the two, thus making peace, and in this one body to reconcile both of them to God through the cross, by which he put to death their hostility. (Ephesians 2:11–16)

We are left with this concluding question: Can we, should we, *will* we choose to agree with our God?

Postscript

Dear Reader, as this book was about to be published, the genocidal attack on Israel struck on October 7, 2023, a match that has ignited a huge conflagration. After the initial horror over its brutality, Israel's fear of another Holocaust brought a strong response, a reprisal so militarily superior and causing so much destruction as to turn public opinion once again against Israel and Jews.

A New Round of Polarization

Soon, outsiders divided up into partisan camps. Some are most concerned about the position Israel finds herself in, and others are identifying more strongly with her neighbors' plight. Even on American streets and college campuses marchers began shouting "from the River to the Sea" (i.e., the Jordan to the Mediterranean—that is, wiping out the whole of Israel). Infiltrated revolutionaries escalate the rhetoric, voicing clear intents: "Death to the Jews!"

Only eighty-some years ago the horror of the Holocaust elicited a determined commitment voiced as "Never again!" Has the world forgotten the Jewish peoples' near extermination in Europe in our own generation? History's complicated backdrop seems to be ignored by those who have been programed to think in Marxist terms, in the mantras of class conflict—in just two categories: oppressors and oppressed.

Scriptural Illiteracy

When a culture becomes biblically illiterate, it shrinks down to the present. It loses the Scriptures' wider perspectives of past history and future expectations. Secularism dwells on the current. Relying on digital sources tends to shrivel the majority of people's perspectives down to their screens, to the now, even to the minute. Having never considered, or else denied, what has happened between Jews and Gentiles throughout history, many watchers are limited to whatever the media presents on the screen. The wider hostilities engulfing Israel are scarcely fathomed by an average viewer.

Today's warring chapter is inherited from age-long struggles recorded in the Bible between Isaac and Ishmael, Jacob and Esau, the Hebrews and Pharoah, Judah and Babylon, Israel and Rome, and AD history up to today. We can empathize with both Israel's and the Muslim community's yearnings, for the sins of the past have caught these cousins in a perpetual cycle of offense, revenge, and retaliation.

Who Is the David and Who Is the Goliath?

On a screen picturing a current moment, tanks look bigger than rocket launchers. Yet, if we would view this sad chapter through a wider lens, history and geography show little Israel to be the David, not the Goliath. Israel is surrounded by monolithic countries openly vowing to exterminate her. Jews are fighting for the right to exist.

We could view this struggle through various lenses. Seen through the biblical story, David was a small victor over big Goliath. Understanding the story truly, it was not little David who won over huge Goliath; it was not his stone, but David's faith in God enabled it. Seen through history, Jews were an unwelcome minority repeatedly exiled out of majority populations. Seen through the Holocaust, emaciated Jews perished in massive crematoriums. Seen in today's media, Israeli tanks look big; Gaza rocks/rockets look small. Seen on a map, Israel is a re-sented peoples' small island of refuge in a massive Muslim sea.

Implications, Deceptions, Manipulations, Confusions

Christendom and Islam have both set the scene for this to happen, each in their own way. Christians are implicated by a preponderance of replacement theology that has yielded a history of contempt for Jews. What is happening now grows out of Christendom's twisted history with Israel, the subject matter of this book's preceding chapters. Ishmael's and Esau's descendants continue to sustain ill will against the descendants of Abraham, Isaac, and Jacob. After the AD 600s, monolithic hostility against any faith except Islam was born.

The convergence of all this animosity produces wide re-percussions. European Christendom's two-thousand-year Jew hatred leaves Israel in an unbearable position. The Middle East's religious teachings manipulate Gaza into an impossible plight. The secular world is up for grabs in this polarization. The media's handling of the conflict can easily manipulate pub-lic opinion.

Islam is a puzzlement to most Westerners watching the news and aching for those suffering in Gaza, and Israel as well. How could such a lethal situation have befallen both of these peoples? The sad reality is that the Muslim-taught worldview rejects the sovereign choice made by God. Islam's stated goal is to replace the One who has revealed himself in Scripture with another one introduced six hundred years after the Messiah's Incarnation. Jews and Christians are seen as the stumbling blocks whom Islam is committed to either eliminate or bring into subjection under worldwide rule.

Biblical Enlightenment

What can the Scriptures tell us about this situation? The world's Creator chose one little community as his launching pad, his prototype. He would reveal himself to them. Their history together with him would encompass profound relationships and would gift them with moral and spiritual principles. But their unbelief time after time proved rampant, and faithfulness to the God of the Covenant repeatedly would only remain in a remnant of the whole community.

When the Lord Jesus' Incarnation took place, God's revelation of his heart was extended from the prototype to all the world. Despite the resurrection's proof of *Yeshua's* identity, Christendom's history seems to have mirrored Israel's saga of pledging faith to the LORD, then turning to both old and new idols, being warned, being disciplined, being forgiven, reforming, and then falling again into ignoring or even hating God. Faithfulness to the Incarnated Lord Jesus and his Word keeps being found in only small remnants of Christians across the world.

The Judeo/Christian understanding is that God is the world's rightful sovereign. Those who hold Israel dear do so because of his love, not theirs. He avows his eternal love of his covenant people over and over in Scripture. Jesus believers' respect for the chosen people is deep because it is the Jews who gave Christians the Patriarchs, the Scriptures, and the Savior of the entire world—both Jewish and Gentile.

The demonic nature of the October 7th attack graphically demonstrated Satan's perpetual warfare against the Creator and all who somehow represent the God of Abraham, Isaac, and Jacob, i.e., Jews and Christians. Satan-inspired attacks on Jews throughout history are well documented. Furthermore, today's secular media seems strangely silent about millions of the world's Christians who are being persecuted, disenfranchised, imprisoned, burned out, driven out, and martyred today, more than in all centuries before.

Humble Assessment and Confession of Guilt

Rather than choosing up sides or making unexamined judg-
ments, those from Christendom's background should be griev-
ing. About what? First, about God's chosen instrument, Israel,
and her adversaries all suffering so fiercely; and second, for the
Church's wrongdoings toward Israel that have compounded
over the centuries. It was guilt for the persecutions of the past,
capped by the Holocaust, which led to Israel being allowed to
try to exist in one small refuge, the Hebrews' original homeland, a New-Jersey-sized area surrounded by a geographically
vast array of avowed enemies. Immediately, the British reneged
on their former initiative. Although established as a state in
1948, Israel has been attacked by her surrounding neighbors
repeatedly. She is even denied existence by the Palestinian char-
ter, but has nowhere else to go except, as genocidally chanted,
"into the sea."

Contemplating Our World's Future

Jesus told us that in humanity's fallen condition, wars and ru-
mors of wars were to be expected. They point to the only source
of the world's rescue—the return of the Savior, the promised
Prince of Peace. Only God knows the truth of history's saga. We
wonder how this current chapter of the chosen peoples' pilgrimage relates to where we are in history. God has disciplined his
sinful people over and over through evil empires. We wonder
where today's historical impasse fits in to his overall purposes.
How is this war impacting Israel's various factions? Will more
and more Jewish people come to the Savior who their God sent
to them and all the world? Will the Church confess her sins and
be renewed in our times? Will God's Spirit increasingly move
among Muslim communities in surprising ways? Might some
secularists be shaken out of their spiritual poverty?

Deliverance?

Humanly speaking there is little hope for conviction, admission, repentance, and renewal, since humanity has proven that despite our education and advancements, we are unable to save ourselves. *Shalom* in human hearts must precede cultural *Shalom*. Jesus is the divine Deliverer sent to redeem anyone willing to accept God's offer of forgiveness. At the end of the Bible, Jesus is revealed as the Bridegroom who promises that at the end of this chapter of world history, he will come for his ethnically varied Bride and re-create a new heaven and earth, one rejoicing in love, righteousness, and peace.

It took the Incarnation for God to intervene from outside to provide redemption. It also will take his intervention from outside to bring the world's perpetual tragedies to an end. Who is it who both promises and can fulfill what humanity needs? Only God can provide forgiveness and redemption from our sins. The Prince of Peace is the only One able to deliver humanity from our perpetual cycles of revenge and retaliation. Who else offers peace to the whole world with no distinctions? Only the Savior equally loves all whom he created. He is the bridge between Jews and the nations.

Two Final Thoughts

This postscript, written in light of the present-day Middle East tragedy, is an attempt to frame some concluding statement. However, these thoughts are simply one person's opinions. God-honest Truth is what we need. So, not trusting in my limited conclusions, I think it best to simply share two final points, one tied to the preceding chapters as they pertain to the present, and one related to the future.

First, considering the current crisis, lest Christians in the wider world stand in uninformed or arrogant judgment on either of these two warring peoples, let us remember that it was the accumulated sins of Christendom that put God's chosen people in this unsolvable position. Let us empathize with everyone who is suffering and pray for all who need to awaken to God's perpetually offered forgiveness and restoration. May each of us try to discern and fulfill our own calling in relationship to the outworking of God's eternal goal.

Dear Reader, a second concern: in light of eternity, people choose to either reject or accept God's message to humanity as recorded in God's revealed Word. The One in whom all authority is found has given us clues about how he will bring history as we know it to a close, before he fulfills his promise to renew the world in love and righteousness. Do consider two pertinent predictions of what to expect and prepare for, truths which the Lord Jesus has given to us. Examine and take seriously his warnings about the Day of judgment each of us will face, as described by the Savior in Matthew 24 and 25. Then, anticipate his promises to those Jews and Gentiles who respond to his merciful love as glimpsed in Revelation 21 and 22. Contemplate the magnificent future described in the Bridegroom's last recorded words to his beloved world.

Dear Readers who may find yourselves unwilling to investigate the truth that God has uniquely given us in his Word, I can only ask, *Oh Jew, Oh Gentile, Why?*

Ω

Supportive Ministries

Chosen People Ministries.
241 East 51st St.
New York, NY 10022–6502

Friends of Israel Gospel Ministry
P.O. Box 908
Bellmawr, NJ 08099

Israel My Glory
(Friends of Israel's bi-monthly magazine)
P.O. Box 908
Bellmawr, NJ 08099

Jews for Jesus
60 Height Street
San Francisco, CA 94102–5895

Jewish Voice Ministries International
P.O. Box 31998
Phoenix, AZ 85046–1998

Messianic Jewish Alliance of America.
P.O. Box 274
Springfield, PA 19064–0274

Olive Tree Ministries
P.O. Box 1452
Maple Grove, MN 55311–6452

TJCII: Toward Jerusalem Council II
6304 Belt Line Rd.
Dallas, TX 75254

Union of Messianic Congregations
P.O. Box 360075
Melbourne, FL 32936

Bibliography of Resources

Archbold, Norma Parish. *The Mountains of Israel: The Bible and the West Bank*, 4th ed. Jerusalem: Phoebe's Song, 2008.

Barth, Markus. *Israel and the Church: Contribution to a Dialogue for Peace*. Richmond: John Knox, 1969.

Bascom, Charles, and Kay Bascom. *The Messiah Mystery: The Old and New Testaments' Inseparable Disclosure*. La Vergne, TN: Lightning Source, 2006.

Bascom, Kay. *Jubilee Journey*. Lowville, NY: Olive Press, 2021.

———. *Overcomers*. Germany: Verlag für Kultur und Wissenschaft, 2018; Eugene, OR: Wipf & Stock, 2018.

Bernis, Jonathan. "Roadblocks to Redemption." *Jewish Voice Today*, Sep/Oct (2008) 5–6.

Cahn, Jonathan. *The Book of Mysteries*. Lake Mary, FL: Charisma, 2016.

———. *The Return of the Gods*. Lake Mary, FL: Charisma, 2022.

Carrol, James. *Constantine's Sword: The Church and the Jews*. Boston: Houghton Mifflin, 2001.

Collins, Larry, and Dominique Lapierre. *O Jerusalem*. New York: Pocket Books, 1973.

Flannery, Edward H. *The Anguish of the Jews: Twenty-Three Centuries of Antisemitism*. Mahwah, NJ: Paulist, 1985.

Forbush, William Byron, ed. *Fox's Book of Martyrs*. Philadelphia: John C. Winston Company, 1926.

Halevi, Yossi Klein. *Letters to My Palestinian Neighbor*. New York: Harper Collins, 2018.

———. *Like Dreamers*. New York: Harper Collins, 2013.

Hefley, James, and Marti Hefley. *Arabs, Christians, Jews*. Plainfield, NJ: Logos International, 1978.

Hilberg, Raul. *The Destruction of the European Jews*. Eastford, CT: Martino Fine Books, 2019.

Horner, Barry E. *Future Israel: Why Christian Anti-Judaism Must Be Challenged*. Nashville, TN: B&H, 2007.

Israel My Glory, bi-monthly magazine. Friends of Israel Gospel Ministry, Bellmawr, N J.

Jocz, Jakob. *The Jewish People and Jesus Christ after Auschwitz: A Study of the Controversy between Church and Synagogue*. Grand Rapids: Baker, 1981.

Jones, A. H. M. *Constantine and the Conversion of Europe*. London: English University Press, 1961.

Kinzer, Mark S. *Jerusalem Crucified, Jerusalem Risen: The Resurrected Messiah, the Jewish People, and the Land of Promise*. Eugene, OR: Cascade, an imprint of Wipf & Stock, 2018.

Liberman, Paul, and Jack Wasson. *Don't Call Me Christian*. Arlington, TX: Tishbite, 2015.

McDermott, Gerald R. *The New Christian Zionism: Fresh Perspectives on Israel and the Land*. Downers Grove, IL: Intervarsity, 2016.

Messianic Jewish Family Bible Project. *Tree of Life: The New Covenant*. Shippensburg, PA: Destiny Image, 2011.

Messianic Times, bi-monthly magazine serving the International Messianic community. Amherst, N Y.

Metaxas, Eric. *Bonhoeffer*. Nashville: Thomas Nelson, 2010.

————. *Letter to the American Church*. Washington, DC: Salem Books, 2022.

Moreshet Heritage Foundation of America. *Bible Versus Tradition*. Granbury, TX: 2017.

One New Man, docuseries: Rabbit Trail Productions, 2022. http://rabbittrailproductions.com/onenewmanseries.

Ouweneel, Willem J. *The Eternal People: God in Relation to Israel; Post-New Testament Israel*. Vol. 4/1B of An Evangelical Introduction to Reformational Theology. Jordan Station, Ontario: Paideia, 2020.

Peters, Joan. *From Time Immemorial*. Chicago: JKAP, 1984.

Phillips, Melanie. *The World Turned Upside Down*. New York: Encounter, 2010.

Raheb, Mitri. *Faith in the Face of Empire*. Maryknoll, New York: Orbis, 2014.

Saada, Tass. *The Mind of Terror*. Carol Stream, IL: Tyndale, 2016.

Schlink, M. Basilea. *Israel, My Chosen People: A German Confession Before God and the Jews*. Old Tappan, NJ: Chosen, 1988.

Schwartz, Adi, and Einat Wilf. *The War of Return*. New York: St. Martin's, 2020.

Stern, David H. *Complete Jewish Bible*. Clarksville, MD: Jewish New Testament Publications, 1998.

————. *Messianic Jewish Manifesto*. Jerusalem: Jewish New Testament Publications, 1988.

————. *Restoring the Jewishness of the Gospel*. Jerusalem: Jewish New Testament Publications, 1988.

Tishby, Noa. *Israel: A Simple Guide to the Most Misunderstood Country on Earth*. New York: Free Press, an imprint of Simon and Schuster, 2021.

Trueman, Carl R. *Strange New World*. Wheaton, IL: Crossway, 2022.

Verduin, Leonard. *The Reformers and Their Stepchildren*. Sarasota, FL: The Christian Hymnary, 1991.

Wilson, Marvin R. *Our Father Abraham*. Grand Rapids: Eerdmans, 1989.

Wolff, Robert F. *Unity: Awakening the One New Man*. Chambersburg, PA: Drawbaugh, 2011.

Yousef, Mosab Hassan. *Son of Hamas*. Carol Stream, IL: Tyndale, 2010.

www.ingramcontent.com/pod-product-compliance
Lightning Source LLC
Chambersburg PA
CBHW071830090426
42737CB00012B/2220